FITTING IN

FOUR GENERATIONS OF COLLEGE LIFE

Barbara A. Schreier

DISCARD

Chicago Historical Society

The exhibition *Fitting In: Four Generations of College Life* was organized by the Chicago Historical Society and was on view from November 22, 1991 to April 1, 1992.

Published in the United States of America 1991
by the Chicago Historical Society
©1991 by the Chicago Historical Society

Director of Publications: Russell Lewis
Edited by Patricia Bereck Weikersheimer
  and Claudia Lamm Wood
Designed by Bill Van Nimwegen
Composed in ITC Century Light and Book Condensed with Lubalin Graph Bold running feet and initials on a Macintosh IIci using Quark Xpress 3.0. Printed by Great Lakes Graphics, Inc., Skokie, Illinois

Cover photograph by James Bixby. Courtesy of Northwestern University Archives.

Library of Congress Cataloging-in-Publication Data

Schreier, Barbara A.
     Fitting in: four generations of college life /
     by Barbara A. Schreier
          p. cm.
     Includes bibliographical references and index.
     ISBN 0-913820-16-4 : $12.95
     1. College students—United States—Social life and
        customs—History—20th century. 2. Women
        college students—United States—Social life and
        customs—History—20th century. I. Title.
     LA229.S318 1991
     378.1'98'0973—dc20   91-34632
                                                      CIP

Contents

Fitting In: Four Generations of College Life
has been made possible through the extraordinary generosity of:

The Costume Committee of the Chicago Historical Society

Major support has also been provided by:

Editel Chicago

Hartmarx Corporation

Mr. and Mrs. William D. Ross

Mr. and Mrs. Patrick G. Ryan

The Siragusa Foundation

Mrs. Howard L. Willett, Jr.

Additional gifts have been received from:

Jostens

Mr. and Mrs. Daniel R. Lee

Universal Recording Corporation

Lili Ann and Richard Zisook,
Morrie and Shirlee Mages Foundation

Foreword

itting In: Four Generations of College Life is the first major exhibition organized by the Chicago Historical Society's curator of costumes, Barbara Schreier, since she joined the Society's staff in September 1990. Both the exhibition and this catalogue are characterized by an engaging presentation of new scholarship on a subject many of us have "studied" firsthand.

The subject of college life seems appropriate for Barbara to examine. She moved to Chicago from Amherst, Massachusetts, where she was a professor at the University of Massachusetts for nine years. There she not only observed today's college students from the perspective of a historian, but she also taught classes on the history of costume, changing relationships between men and women, and social history.

Barbara has, in previous exhibition projects, examined some intriguing issues about clothing and what it means to the wearer. In 1984, she surveyed the collection of the Chrysler Museum and selected pieces that reflected traditional models of femininity for the exhibition, *Mystique and Identity*. She later served as a contributing curator and coauthor of the accompanying book for *Men and Women*, the Smithsonian's groundbreaking exhibition about fashion and gender. Both of these exhibitions paved the way for her study of a century of college life and fashion.

While preparing *Fitting In*, Barbara frequently told me about a great find—a wrapper that allowed a student of the 1890s freedom of movement in her dorm room, a pair of white bucks from the 1940s that a distinguished Chicago lawyer had been convinced to part with, or a monumental pink plastic beehive, which today's coeds would never recognize as a hair dryer. The pieces themselves may be modest, but they each have a story to tell. The challenge for Barbara, as for every curator, is to bring these objects to life so that they may tell their stories. *Fitting In* succeeds particularly well in combining research in traditional sources with artifacts. The exhibition will interest scholars of both costume and social history and will make that scholarship accessible to a general audience.

Visitors to the exhibition and readers of the catalogue will find that *Fitting In* is quite different from most previous costume exhibitions at the Chicago

Historical Society. It is about the lives of the women and men who attended college in the 1890s, 1920s, 1940s, and 1960s more than about the style of clothing itself. The fashions are used as primary sources to provide information about the lives of college students. Costumes are combined with other objects, such as a hip flask and a Frisbee, and archival material, such as letters and scrapbooks, to capture the essence of the college experience.

Barbara brings the past to life masterfully. The portraits of each generation ring true to me; I find myself remembering not only my own college history, with political strikes and flowing Indian-print dresses, but also my mother's stories of gray flannel skirts worn during the postwar years and my grandmothers' pride at attending college to train as teachers.

While memory is used to engage us in the topic of college life, the exhibition takes us beyond a nostalgic look at old college days. Perhaps because we never thought of our student selves as a subject of study, the exhibition yields some surprising insights. For each generation, the college experience seems fresh and unique. The process of inventing a life-style is a creative act. When the choices are reinforced by peers in the form of fashions and fads, students feel that their new way is a good way.

Despite the differences in styles and politics, it is the continuity of the college experience that is most striking. Whether flappers or hippies, each generation of college students provides a supportive community of peers where a student can experiment with costumes and roles while inventing his or her adult self. College grants this freedom while giving clear signals about how to fit in. It is this element of college life that remains constant.

Memory is a powerful tool for engaging people in the consideration of the past. In inviting us to see ourselves and beyond, Professor Schreier teaches us some important lessons about ourselves and our society over the last century.

Susan Page Tillett
Director of Curatorial Affairs
Chicago Historical Society

Donors and Lenders

Mrs. Todd Abrams

Mrs. Thomas Hoban Alcock

Hon. Wayne R. Andersen

Amy Waller Anderson

Mrs. Robert Gardner Anderson

Mr. and Mrs. Henry X Arenberg

Mrs. Bernard Iddings Bell

Estate of Mrs. Alonzo Benn

Michael Biddle

Mr. and Mrs. William Biddle

Mrs. Edward S. Block

Mrs. Philip Block, Jr.

Mrs. Frances Bosca

Mrs. Edwin Brand III

Mrs. F. L. Bruno

Ruth Moss Buck

Mr. Gabe Burton

Paul J. Darling

Mrs. George Davison

Mrs. Edith DeMar

Mary Derby

Jo Hopkins Deutsch

Mrs. William Warren Dixon

Dr. George F. Eisenbrand

Evanston Historical Society

Lucy Fairbank

Lester E. Frankenthal III

Jack R. Franks

Mrs. Oscar Gerber

Harriet Rosenfeld Gershman

Mr. and Mrs. Walter Gieseke

Nancy Gorman

Kate Gregg

Rosemary Hale

Mrs. D. D. Hamacheck

Alan Hammerman

Estate of Anna Emery Hanson

Hartmarx Corporation

Mrs. Frank P. Hixon

Mrs. Arthur Hoffheimer

Aravia L. Holloman

Mrs. James M. Hopkins

Mrs. Edward N. Hurley, Jr.

Mrs. Ernest L. Ives

Mrs. David Sawyer Jennings

Mr. Virgil Johnson

Jostens

Mrs. Edward B. Kelley

Mrs. James S. Kemper

Mr. Jack Kirkby

Miss Ramona Koenamann

Dr. Kate Hirschberg Kohn

Miss Hannah E. Krueger

Estate of Margaret M. Kruty

Miss Elizabeth Krutz

Mrs. Walter K. Krutz

Mr. and Mrs. Eugene Kwas

Lake Forest College

Sylvia Landsman

Andrew Leo

Nancy Lerman

Janet Lerman-Graff

Russell Lewis

Mrs. Howard Linn

Mrs. Otto Madlener

Perry Marks

Mrs. Frank D. Mayer

Donald Metzger

Mrs. Russell J. McCaughey

Mr. Brooks McCormick, Jr.

Mrs. George B. McKibbin

Katherine McMillan

Mrs. C. Phillip Miller

Mrs. Ralph J. Mills, Jr.

Minette-Bates, Inc.

Mary Minow

Mr. and Mrs. Newton N. Minow

Ralph Geoffrey Newman

Mr. Paul R. Nordskog

Mrs. Lawrence F. Norem

Northwestern University

Mrs. Robert G. Peck

Donald and Nancy Peterson

Mrs. Judy Rasin

Mrs. Milton D. Ratner

James Reinhardt

Walter Reinhardt

Mrs. Sanger P. Robinson

Mrs. Walter L. Ross II

Mrs. William Ross

Frank Rossi

Saks Fifth Avenue/Nena Ivon

Nancy Salomon

Daniel R. Santow

Arthur Schreier

Mr. and Mrs. Thomas Schreier

Schwinn History Center

Peter Seltzer

Dr. Clement M. Silvestro

Eugene Siskel

Mrs. Sumner S. Sollitt

Mrs. K. P. Smith

Sharon Smith

F. William Spiegel, Jr.

Mr. and Mrs. Gardner H. Stern

Mrs. Jules N. Stiffel

Mrs. Frank L. Sulzberger

Susan Page Tillett

University of Chicago

Genevieve Urbain

Larry A. Viskochil

Mrs. Thatcher Waller

Miss Estelle F. Ward

Mrs. Edward R. Weed

Mrs. John P. Welling

Mrs. Robert C. Woolard

Mr. and Mrs. Philip K. Wrigley

Acknowledgments

xhibitions at the Chicago Historical Society are team efforts, and I had the good fortune to work with an extraordinarily talented team. A tight schedule meant that I had to rely on a group of research assistants for much of the legwork. Mary Curran and Lesley Martin searched through numerous university archives with expert eyes and unearthed hundreds of facts and images. Donna Pleiter, Janet Lawrence, and Colleen Sullivan found creative answers for the many research questions that I posed to them. Archivists and librarians at the University of Illinois, Library of Congress, University of Illinois, Loyola University, North Park College, Mundelein College, Vassar College, George Washington University, Bryn Mawr College, and Yale University were especially helpful. Wilma Slaight and Jean Berry, both of Wellesley College, and Marjorie Sly of Smith College merit special mention. Thanks also go to Shelly Foote and Spencer Crew of the Smithsonian Institution for their willingness to share photographic research with me. I am most grateful to Patrick Quinn, archivist at Northwestern University, who offered unlimited assistance.

The costume staff at the Society deserves much of the credit for this exhibition. Costume conservator Terri Edwards, with the assistance of Lee Ann Rose, gave many of the costumes a new life, and Cathy Olson's unstinting support as curatorial assistant proved invaluable. Her talents in dressing mannequins are evident in the color photographs of this catalogue. The support of Susan Samek, assistant costume curator, guided me through the entire process. She assumed a Herculean share of the department's responsibilities so that I could concentrate on this catalogue.

Carol von Stade, whose efforts resulted in a substantial portion of the exhibition's funding, embraced this project with her usual vitality and great humor. The Costume Committee has continued its marvelous tradition of support for the department by pledging a generous gift of one hundred thousand dollars. My thanks go to chairman Lawrie Weed for her leadership and fund-raising efforts.

Society staff members Lisa Bendoff, Janice McNeill, Claire Cass, Diane Ryan, Robert Goler, and Corey Seeman located artifacts in their collections for the exhibition. Special thanks also go to Louise Brownell, registrar, and Carol Turchan, conservator. Susan Page Tillett, director of curatorial affairs, believed in this project from the beginning, and she ran interference whenever I needed her help. Society president Ellsworth Brown has expressed his enthusiasm and support for this new interpretation of social history through costume since I first met him two years ago.

The photographic skills and artistic talents of John Alderson and Jay Crawford enrich this catalogue. The design department breathed life into my ideas, and the catalogue and exhibition are richer for the designers' and preparators' suggestions. Special thanks go to Bill Van Nimwegen for his creative design of the catalogue and his steady good humor in working with a new curator. I am very grateful to Ted Gibbs, Myron Freedman, and Walter Reinhardt for sharing their time and talents so generously.

I am indebted to Andrew Leo, whose ideas shaped the initial conception of the exhibition. As exhibition consultant, James Sims asked the right questions, and his visual skills and interpretive talents gave the project its purpose. If the relationship between a curator and designer is like a marriage, I never want a divorce; Michael Biddle is a remarkable designer, and his talents saturate every inch of the exhibition space.

To Valerie Steele, Ellen Hughes, and Russell Lewis, I offer my appreciation for their careful reading of the manuscript. The catalogue is stronger because of their intellectual acuity. Claudia Lamm Wood provided me with editorial support and helped see the project through to completion. I am most grateful to Patricia Bereck Weikersheimer, project editor, who possesses the rare ability to bring a reader's perspective to a manuscript.

This exhibition required an extensive collecting initiative, and thanks go to all of the individuals who donated or lent objects. Simply stated, this exhibition would not have been possible without their generosity. Jo Minow took a special interest in the project, and her willingness to share personal memories helped me find the student voice for the 1940s. Tom and Doris Schreier helped their daughter track down obscure sources in used bookstores. Ellen Ross took her responsibilities as Costume Committee acquisitions chairman to heart, and many of the artifacts on display are a direct result of her efforts. A special acknowledgment goes to Henry X Arenberg; if there was a title of honorary curator, it would go to Hank.

I extend my final thank you to Liv Pertzoff, who convinced me that there is life beyond the classroom. Because of her, I am no longer answering that time-honored question: "Is this going to be on the test?"

Introduction

The need to fit in, to find a place among peers, is universal. Yet at certain times this yearning takes on exaggerated importance; adolescence and young adulthood are such times. Emotionally vulnerable, youths struggle with questions of Who am I? and Who do I want to be? The answers may be uncertain, but clearly the path to discovery rests with peers, not parents.

Going away to college has come to symbolize breaking away from parents. Insulated from the economic consequences of the adult world, undergraduates enjoy the luxury of a four-year transitional cocoon. College students create a youth-oriented subculture in which the members are united by attitudes and circumstances. In the flush of their newfound independence, collegians work at inventing a life-style. Unconcerned with the complexity of self-realization, they seize upon the fashions and fads that promise instant transformation and acceptance. The imperative of fitting in magnifies even the smallest fashion detail.

Throughout these four years of self-conscious exploration, the gaze of peers acts as the critical mirror. As students wonder, How do I look?, they constantly measure themselves against this reflected image. The group, in turn, measures them with a demanding eye. The tribal college community judges individuals to see who rates and who does not. Peers sort themselves out with breathtaking speed, often relying on clothing as the critical predictor. Letter sweaters and plastic pocket protectors forever separate the jocks from the nerds. The sartorial chasm between the social butterfly and the grind is equally pronounced.

Campus priorities and pressures shape both the *Fitting In* exhibition and catalogue. Their intention is to tell the story of four generations of college life from the student's perspective. Examinations and classroom lectures are noticeably absent; instead, collegians' experiences reveal the life students created for themselves.

The inspiration for *Fitting In* came from the college wardrobe of a young Chicago woman, Jessie Clara Ward. Leaving home in 1894 to attend the Capen-Burnham School in Northampton, Massachusetts, Jessie packed a wardrobe made for her by a dressmaker. This educational adventure required silk gowns, woolen gymnasium bloomers, a walking suit, and a new dormitory wrapper. Due to the generosity of her niece, Estelle F. Ward, these garments are now part of the Chicago Historical Society's costume collection.

When Jessie Ward went to school, a college education was a rare privilege, especially for women. How would the experiences of a turn-of-the-century graduate compare to those of subsequent generations of collegians? The search for answers resulted in an exploration of undergraduate life in the 1890s, 1920s, 1940s, and late 1960s. Separated by twenty years, the youths who once

asserted their own campus independence became the parents of the next generation of collegians.

The collective history of these four groups is cyclical rather than evolutionary. While coming of age certainly involves testing limits and searching for a community of peers, it does not always lead to rebellion. Revolt can turn as sour as accommodation. These four generations each benefited from the cloistered world of campus life, but they still reflected the social climate of their times. They were insulated from, but not immune to, outside events. Sometimes the search for independence set students on a collision course with the dominant culture—students of the 1920s and the 1960s, for example, defined themselves through their alienation and conflict with those in power. In other periods, however, collegians found their identity within the framework of mainstream values. During the

1890s and the 1940s, undergraduates and educators worked out an easy balance of power. But regardless of whether students act as agents of change or of convention, they must answer to their peers.

In the late nineteenth century, higher education for women was still a grand experiment, and its promoters had to accommodate cultural assumptions about a woman's proper place and special needs. Creating structured environments that resembled well-ordered, secluded households, educators committed themselves to protecting students' moral and physical development. Female students accepted the situation as a logical extension of Victorian society. They also, however, delighted in opportunities to escape the trappings of proper womanhood within the safety of the all-female communities. Along with formal wools and fancy silks, turn-of-the-century collegians packed shirtwaists, tailored skirts, and gymnasium suits in their college trunks. These educational pioneers wore the emblems of the "new woman" with pride.

The expanding numbers of college students in the twentieth century shattered the delicate balance between students and administrators. Confronted with the growing army of outspoken students who were in the forefront of the nationwide youth culture, college authorities recognized the limits of their power. But they were unprepared for the assault of 1920s undergraduates. Existing rules and regulations faltered as college students first tested and then openly defied standards of behavior. Undergraduates dismissed existing values as irrelevant. Women bobbed their hair, raised their hemlines, and spoke of sex candidly. Men snuggled up to their partners on the dance floor and

in the back seats of automobiles. Students competed with each other for the best lines, both verbally and sartorially. Celebrated as the most visible representatives of the modern generation, students reshaped the moral contours and the appearance of society.

The sobering realities of the depression and World War II overshadowed, but did not extinguish, the self-conscious testing of youth. Wartime students still wanted the insulated pleasures of college life, but administrators rarely had to contend with overt or hostile rebellion. Peers monitored behavior far more closely than the administration ever could have. At a time when college women far outnumbered college men, sororities assumed the decisive role in enforcing social norms. Sisters formally codified dress regulations in their house rules and informally established expectations through example. They made it clear that the youthful styles of saddle shoes and dungarees had their place, as did formal gowns. Following their parents' clothing logic, students dressed appropriately for all occasions.

Students and administrators clashed again in the late 1960s. Like the youths who revolted in the 1920s, the undergraduates of the 1960s demanded control of their lives, and the force of a collective voice strengthened their position. But while the flapper and her male counterpart concentrated on the personal issues of smoking, drinking, dancing, and dating, youths in the sixties filtered their demands through a prism of politics. They turned the emptiness of fashion against itself; clothing became a weapon against materialism and consumerism. Dressed in the uniform of protest— jeans, peace signs, and love beads—these students wanted to change not only the campus but the world.

Although the contrasts among these four generations are striking, the similarities are equally rich in meaning. Regardless of place or time, newly arrived freshmen struggle with the daily challenges and frustrations of adjustment. Letters written to parents in the 1890s asking for more money or packages of food sound remarkably like the plaintive requests of students seventy years later. So, too, does the students' preoccupation with dress. The difference between fitting in or hopelessly standing out can rest on an inch of hemline or on the flare of a trouser. College styles fluctuate wildly, but the importance of dress as vestments of initiation remains constant.

Small Acts of Defiance:
College Women at the Turn of the Century

Nineteenth-century society drew absolute boundaries around men's and women's lives. Men dominated and directed the public world of work; women guided, nurtured, and protected the private spaces of home. The domestic sphere celebrated female virtue, morality, and piety. But what of a woman's intellect? Mid-century educators argued that learning could enhance the code of true womanhood. With an educated woman at its helm, the home would become the center of inspiration and learning. If necessary, educated women could work as schoolteachers before marriage. Women thus gained a foothold in the academic community without upsetting the delicate gender balance.

Soon, however, a new set of expectations developed among women. Some collegians grew frustrated by societal limits. Bolstered by the pleasures of intellectual inquiry and inspired by the late nineteenth-century reform movements, graduates from the 1870s and 1880s began to reevaluate the status of women. Significantly, they also became the educators of the next generation of female collegians. Bearing the imprint of traditional values, they committed themselves to shaping new educational patterns and opportunities for women.

Women with the means and ambition to attend college in the 1890s entered a supportive and enclosed environment. Whether in the segregated environment of single-sex colleges or, to a lesser extent, in the separate areas women carved out for themselves at coeducational schools, this isolation provided students with a unique opportunity. Rejecting the societal rules that confined women to a narrow life, educators designed welcoming havens. Removed from the public eye, students could explore the question of women's legitimate place on campus and in the outside world.[1]

College women in the 1890s entered a sheltered atmosphere where they could explore their place in the world and make their own decisions. Opposite, a student at Illinois State Normal School addresses her studies. Above left, Wellesley students gather to make daisy chains. In the privacy of a dorm room, women could shed their restrictive clothing and relax with friends.

This dressing gown and matching slippers, above right and middle, would have provided a welcome change after a day in corsets and high-topped, lace-up shoes.

Sandwiched between the larger issues of values, friendships, and learning were the smaller decisions that students confronted daily. Should I shorten my bicycle skirt? Can I try out for the play? These explorations had limits, and the testing process created its own set of tensions, since the answers had to be measured against administrative policy, societal pressures, and parental expectations. Yet the freedom to challenge old precepts proved liberating.

Poised at a historic moment of great change and social upheaval, collegiate women of the 1890s helped to redefine the college experience. They understood that the social part of their education was the richest part. Only one's classmates could fully appreciate the pangs of homesickness, the frustrations of a tyrannical professor, or the monotony of school food. As students searched for both a personal and professional identity, the community of campus peers became a crucial source of support and affirmation.

Together, students increasingly challenged some aspects of college life. These were small acts of defiance—hosting illicit parties after 10:00 P.M., which was against policy, or testing the limits of chaperoning policies.[2] Their collective voice, however, strengthened the tone of resistance. Individual objections to social regulations, dormitory restrictions, or academic policy developed into group challenges. Educators did not always modify their positions, but they listened. By the beginning of the twentieth century, schools and universities acknowledged students' right to respond to, and participate in, the governance of their lives.

Very few women in the 1890s attended college. Only 4 percent of the population between ages eighteen and twenty-one were enrolled in colleges and universities. Women represented 40 percent of the total college population, and they composed 24 percent of those students enrolled in the regular colleges.[3]

Women students transformed their often drab dorm rooms into cozier quarters where students gathered to socialize (above left). This Wellesley dorm room of 1891 (below left) exhibits many popular decorative items, such as floral fabrics, pillows, and photographs.

Below left, women were members of the first class at Columbian College, which would become George Washington University. Below right, Smith College students, c. 1895, enjoy a rarebit prepared in a chafing dish. A chafing dish was considered an essential accessory of college life.

College women were overwhelmingly white, Protestant, and middle class.[4] The democratic campus spirit that characterized colleges of the period was possible largely because the population was so homogeneous. While colleges claimed that the rich and the poor were alike welcome, and campus officials rarely issued overt statements of discrimination, administrators made it clear in various ways that students of different racial, ethnic, and religious backgrounds would be more comfortable elsewhere.[5]

Under the leadership of visionary educators during the post–Civil War period, colleges for women became scholastically comparable to the best men's colleges. While coeducational institutions battled over sex differences in course selection, and elite, private male institutions refused to open their doors to women, the founders of Vassar, Smith, Mount Holyoke, and Wellesley put forth a new vision. In addition to fostering an intellectually stimulating environment, they created a world where women could come together in study, play, and friendship. Twenty years later, collegians reaped the benefits of their predecessors' success; other women's colleges developed, and coeducational institutions broadened their vision of women's education. By the turn of the century, more people had come to accept, if not always approve of, the college-educated woman.

Nowhere was the spirit of shared community more evident than in the residence halls. Protected from the outside world, women formed close and intense friendships within the intimacy of dorm life. Dormitory parlors provided women with an appropriate setting for public entertaining, but students preferred their own rooms for private socializing. A typical college room of the late 1890s might have included a few rugs scattered on the hardwood floor, a desk, a rocking chair, and a wicker chair.[6] Despite the "pretty furnishings," students were not always delighted. A newcomer to Vassar wrote of her first impressions of her room. On first seeing it, she seized an approaching student: " 'Are you a Freshman? You must come here. You must. My wallpaper is hideous, and there are no pictures . . . on the wall.' . . . In unpacking our trunks . . . we . . . discovered that we liked the same picture above the same dresser, and embraced."[7]

With the addition of "a bureau cover, a few photographs," and some well-placed private possessions, students transformed dorm rooms into artistic sitting rooms. Japanese screens separated the space generally shared by two girls and kept the beds out of view. Roommates cluttered the room with an astonishing array of memorabilia, filling any bare space with pictures, calendars, college pennants, and postcards. The *Chicago Tribune* in 1895 published an account of how women at the University of Chicago personalized the dorm room with its "washstand, a bureau, a couple of chairs, . . . and an iron and brass bed, or a cot." A college girl would "purchase enough crèton to make a loose frilled cover for her bed, which is then heaped with gayly colored cushions until it becomes a seat worthy of the Sultan of Turkey." Also popular were sofa cushions: "Great is the triumph of the girl who can secure the greatest number."[8]

Within this self-contained environment, women could loosen both their corsets and their attitudes while exchanging confidences. Through late-night parties, "high-spirited pranks," and informal food "spreads," women collegians at the turn of the century made life in the residence hall an essential part of the college experience. A University of Chicago coed wrote in her diary of the importance of her friendships and her social life: "Little else going on about the Beatrice [the residence hall], except the walks, talks, after dinner dancing, etc. among the girls, inserted into our busy lives of study, to keep us from turning too mental."[9]

Food starred in these impromptu dormitory events. Defying administrative injunctions to eat only wholesome food at regular hours, collegians indulged in forbidden sweets and chocolates. The nightly feasts at Vassar became so popular that some students organized informal eating clubs, such as "the Nine Nimble Nibblers."[10] While wealthy students arranged elaborately catered teas, most served a variety of chafing dish goodies prepared in their rooms.[11] These rituals became an integral part of the collegiate experience. A Vassar student even exclaimed: "The chafing-dish is the household god of the Freshman. . . . You are at college? Prove it! Produce your chafing-dish!"[12]

Not all students lived on campus. Local boardinghouses, carefully screened by college officials, provided an alternative when the college lacked space or the student lacked money. Yet, the intimacy of dormitory life was clearly the ideal. At urban schools, many students commuted to school, resulting in a fragmented loyalty. Students at the University of Chicago repeatedly lamented the apathy on campus. Attributing the lack of interest to the majority of students who were "day boarders" and who "each afternoon fold their lunch boxes and silently steal away," the campus newspaper offered a remedy: show "this large class of students that outside interests are incompatible with true college life and should be dropped."[13]

Turn-of-the-century collegiate women, especially those at single-sex institutions, developed an elaborate system of campus rituals. By promoting group identity and campus loyalty, these ceremonies marked college as a unique period in a girl's life. The most important customs gave form to a student's place in the hierarchy of academic classes. To one Wellesley freshman, the distinction of wearing the senior cap and gown to chapel and spring ceremonies seemed remote. In a letter home, she wrote: "Wish I were a Senior—don't believe I shall ever get to that dignity."[14]

Within the closed social system of the undergraduate world, college class linked students to a peer group. Class colors, emblems, and pins reinforced these allegiances. By 1920, strong class identification yielded to the power of campus loyalty.[15] Yet, during this period when college traditions were forming, class divisions offered women an identity on campus.

Class allegiance led to class competition in athletics. Fierce rivalries developed, and the annual game between classes drew enthusiastic crowds. The annual class basketball game elicited an outpouring of school spirit. Students came dressed in class colors and everyone sang enthusiastically, because cheering was "not included in the present scheme of womanliness."[16]

Newly founded colleges and universities struggled to keep pace with older institutions by developing their own badges of athletic accomplishment and school spirit. This eagerness prompted one observer to wryly note how quickly a new custom became a tradition with "the sanctity of untold generations behind it."[17] Students looked with favor on the rites and rituals that celebrated the college experience, and they turned to the more established colleges in the East for prototypes.

Campus newspapers spread the message: if traditions do not exist on your campus, borrow them or make them up! Reporting on the practice of honoring varsity athletes with letter sweaters, *The Northwestern* noted that this "custom in vogue in eastern colleges . . . is gradually being adopted by western institutions." The newspaper suggested that while anyone belonging to a university team should be allowed to wear an *N*, only those who have won events in intercollegiate contests should be allowed to wear the cap. "Northwestern should come into line with her sister institutions in the east, on this matter."[18]

Not all campuses, however, were enthusiastic about accepting ready-made traditions. The running commentary that appeared in the 1893 and 1894 editions of the *University of Chicago Weekly* illuminates the frustrations that arose when students disagreed, or did not care, about displays of campus loyalty. The newspaper's constant criticism of the college yell for its lack of "body and meaning" failed to draw an outpouring of school spirit.

While colleges struggled to find appropriate symbols of their emerging identities, students confronted the immediate challenges of their own adjustment to campus life. To help them in this process, they turned to the peer group. Upperclassmen played a crucial role as both models and mentors to freshmen struggling to find their place on campus. In a long-standing tradition at women's colleges, older students served as "sisters" to freshmen, guiding the newcomers through the maze of campus rituals and hosting social events in their honor.[19] On these occasions, the older student acted, and sometimes dressed, the part of the male escort. Every October, Smith sophomores hosted a reception to welcome their younger "sisters." At this formal social occasion, a second-year student would escort a new girl to the party, fill out her dance card, give her flowers, and then see her home.[20]

Loyalties to one's college class developed through rituals and class rivalries. Below, students line up for the Class Day basketball game at Smith, and Wellesley students celebrate the 1889 May Day with a maypole dance.

Such events also took place to a limited extent at coeducational institutions. In 1908, junior women at Cornell staged a mock dormitory wedding of Ima Freshman to Heesa Junior. "Each Freshman arrayed in her 'flossiest togs' was met at the door of the reception hall and escorted up the 'aisle' by a stately Junior in [male] evening dress."[21]

Administrators frowned on this appropriation of men's clothing. Aware of public concerns that education made women less feminine, they feared that public disclosure of the costuming could jeopardize their educational experiment. The women, however, delighted in the opportunity to act the manly part. Instead of meekly submitting to limits imposed by the administration, they created new opportunities for role-playing. Student scrapbooks of the period captured dormitory scenes of high-spirited Halloween parties and makeshift plays with women dressed as male characters. Wearing trousers, boots, and oversized mustaches, students also adopted male postures. Liberated from bodices and petticoats, women cast off the decorous posture of a delicately crossed ankle and a rigid torso. Dressed as men, they sprawled in chairs with their legs spread or stood tall with their hands on their hips.

The most elaborate class traditions surrounded the initiation of freshmen into campus life and the departure of seniors. Every fall, Bryn Mawr freshmen took their legitimate place among their peers on Lantern Night. Dressed in academic robes for the first time, they received a lantern, which symbolized "the light that illumined the way through college life." Later, a mock battle ensued, with sophomores trying to "spirit away" the caps and gowns that the proud freshmen had just purchased.[22] Tree Day at Wellesley marked the freshmen's official acceptance into campus life with the planting of their class tree. At this festival of pageantry and dancing, caps and gowns distinguished the seniors; students of the other classes dressed in "fanciful costumes" in their class colors.[23]

Students enjoyed amateur dramatics as an opportunity for fun and a chance to dress in costumes. Smith women, above left, dress as characters from Alice in Wonderland, *c. 1896. Below left, Vassar sophomores, c. 1908, collect cartloads and armfuls of daisies in preparation for the traditional daisy-chain procession at commencement.*

Opposite, Wellesley sophomores dress as woodsmen, complete with beards. All students wore fanciful costumes to Wellesley's Tree Day, except seniors, who wore caps and gowns.

Students marked the final rite of passage, graduation, with senior auctions, class suppers, and senior plays. At these events, seniors bid their goodbyes and passed on the responsibilities of leadership to the junior class. Vassar celebrated commencement with a daisy-chain procession that became a long-standing tradition. Seniors selected sophomores to carry the chain on Class Day. "The long line of white-robed girls, with the heavy daisy-chain passing over their shoulders and hanging in festoons" honored the graduating seniors in their last days on campus.[24] All of these rituals affirmed the college landscape as a world unto itself. Initiation rites and secret ceremonies drew individuals into a cloistered environment where pageantry and drama celebrated the community of women.

At some coeducational colleges and universities, women relied on sororities to provide these all-important rituals. Originally founded as secret societies, sororities and fraternities gained increasing support among turn-of-the-century students. Since women were often excluded from participating in men's extracurricular organizations, sororities held the promise of a supportive female community on many campuses.[25] They also provided housing on campuses where dormitory space was scarce or nonexistent.

As these clubs grew in number and influence, however, exclusivity and competition sometimes overshadowed the initial goal of democratic fellowship. Student cliques certainly existed on every campus, but Greek-letter societies, with their process of acceptance, codified closed peer groups. Unlike groups such as the YWCA, where interest was the only prerequisite for admission, sororities selected girls who reflected the values of their organization.

Rushing emerged as a testing period of acceptability; for the most status-conscious groups, money and appearance played a crucial part in the evaluation process. When quizzed about the circumstances surrounding a sorority's decision to reject a hopeful aspirant, one student offered the following defense: "Well, they say her people are quite poor now, and if you'd seen the dowdy coat she wore to our evening party I guess you'd have been for turning her down, too."[26]

A senior at a "great co-educational university of the Middle West" elaborated on the unspoken conditions of acceptance. "The 'best' sorority is the one which represents the largest money backing and is formed of girls who make the best appearance in dress and are the most attractive on the ballroom floor." In her candid analysis of the social consequences of not making the grade, she wrote:

> The freshman girl who comes here and is the 'swellest thing,' or who has a 'faculty pull,' or 'loads of money,' finds herself in the thick of the 'rushing.' . . . If she is not found to be of the right stuff, she is dropped at once, and of the many girls who have lavished little courtesies upon her, only a very few continue to be friendly.[27]

Unlike most coeducational schools during this period, the University of Chicago offered women a prominent place in college life. William Rainey Harper, the first president of the university, envisioned the school as the intellectual equivalent of Yale without the elitism. A revised university charter adopted in 1889 stated clearly the equality of male and female students. To fulfill that promise, Harper hired Marion Talbot and Alice Freeman Palmer as deans of women. Trained at eastern all-women colleges and dedicated to the spirit of social reform, these women demanded equal opportunities for their students.[28]

Within the university's progressive environment, women developed a strong tradition of intellectual leadership. But educational autonomy formed only a part of college life. As women in single-sex colleges vividly demonstrated, female collegians had both the need of a social community and the desire to find one's own place among friends. Sororities seemed the answer, but university officials disagreed. Although administrators spoke out against both male and female societies, they viewed sororities as particularly threatening; the Victorian model of proper womanhood demanded cooperation, not competition.

Fearing the worst consequences of elitism and social-class divisiveness, deans Alice Freeman Palmer and Marion Talbot tried to keep sororities out of the University of Chicago. They won the battle but lost the war. Following the model of national organizations, students created their own system of secret clubs, including Quadranglers, Mortar Board, and Wyvern.[29]

This two-piece day dress of rose gauze with its leg-of-mutton sleeves and hourglass shape follows the fashionable silhouette of the mid-1890s.

Sororities and fraternities actively shaped social events at Northwestern University at the turn of the century. Despite the administration's concern about "inter-frat strife" and sorority parties whose ultimate purpose was "a means of display," students turned their backs on the administration and embraced this form of peer selection.[30]

Although higher education contributed to expanding opportunities for the "new woman," cultural prescriptions for proper womanhood in the 1890s still required

College provided opportunities for social contact between men and women. Top, at coeducational institutions, students could meet informally, as at this North Park College wiener roast. Bottom, a dance at Smith College, c. 1897, typifies the more formal dances and promenades at single-sex schools.

piety, chastity, and morality. When parents sent their daughter off to college, they demanded reassurance that these Victorian standards of femininity would be preserved. At both single-sex and coeducational institutions, the burden of propriety fell largely on women's shoulders. Contemporary observers generally acknowledged that "somehow, more is expected of the college girl than of the college boy."[31] While educators struggled to break down the intellectual barriers for women, they needed to maintain the cultural boundaries that protected a woman's reputation. If girls were to remain chaste and pure, their contact with men had to be closely supervised.

Women's colleges clearly had the greatest control in containing the "male presence" on campus. Students had few opportunities for socializing with men; when they did, they were carefully chaperoned. Smith and Vassar students, for example, could invite men to their formal dances, but until the mid-1890s they could not dance with them. Instead, the men "promenaded" or walked with their partners up and down a decorated corridor.[32] At Mount Holyoke, the promenade injunction remained in effect until 1907. No wonder men referred to this festivity as the "eight-mile walk."[33]

Men and women mingled more freely on coeducational campuses. Even though administrators underscored the importance of segregating the sexes by establishing strict chaperoning policies, the environment provided greater opportunities for interaction inside and outside the classroom. *The Northwestern* reported on a sorority-sponsored Halloween party where the girls entertained fraternity boys. "Games were the order of the evening, and proved great fun. Apples, suspended from strings, were consumed to the stem. . . . Dancing was indulged in to a very limited degree."[34]

University of Chicago student Demia Butler, class of 1898, confided in her diary the details of a budding romance. It began when a Mr. Stone walked her home on several occasions. He soon earned the title of "My Knight of the Stoney Heart" because he was "somewhat bashful and reserved"; later, she shortened the nickname to "My Knight." He invited her to skating parties, she included him in the house parties, and they spent afternoons together exploring downtown Chicago. Each event was chaperoned and very proper; yet, the frequency of their interaction could have been possible only at a coeducational school.[35]

As dean of women at the University of Chicago, Marion Talbot assumed the roles of chaperon, adviser, and confessor. When a number of women suggested a sleigh-ride party, she helped organize a group of twenty men and women. After the ride, everyone returned to the women's dorm for cocoa and cake and dancing. On her recommendation, the women insisted that it was a Dutch treat. Talbot explained to her mother, "I told them it would save a good many complications," and the men were "much pleased."[36]

Familiarity between the sexes, however, did not always lead to romance. At the University of Wisconsin and elsewhere, men tended to "import" girls for the Junior Prom and other occasions. They desired "ornamental girls" for these festivities, asking "who wants to spend a lot of money on a girl that he can see every day for nothing?"[37]

If boys spent money on girls, girls certainly spent money on clothing. When Myrtle Whitney went away to Northwestern, she complained to her mother about the rich society girls. Shortly thereafter, she wrote requesting some new clothes, including an elaborate velvet outfit and a lace dress costing thirty dollars. Apparently, Mrs. Whitney agreed to the request but questioned the necessity of fancy dresses for school. Myrtle responded:

As for getting one not trimmed very elaborately. If I have one at all I want a nice one. You know I told you

Despite some observers' concerns that coeducational settings encouraged women to overdress, these Northwestern women enjoyed the pleasures of a mixed outing in shirtwaists and tailored skirts.

that their school dresses were trimmed a great deal. Edith . . . has a new school dress. Nearly half of the waist is velvet, velvet sleeves, and lots of velvet on the skirt. It will be all right to wear to school if it is trimmed.[38]

Many observers blamed coeds' excessive interest in fashion on the presence of men on campus. They accused women of overdressing to impress men. "They wear too big hats and too fine clothes to school and affect a dependent and admiring attitude toward the opposite sex."[39] Hedwig Loeb, who graduated from the University of Chicago in 1902, was clearly the exception. In an English assignment outlining a typical day, she described dressing and fashion as "an ordeal which I would gladly dispense with."[40]

Believing that a "love of dress" distracted students from more important concerns, administrators at all-women colleges expressed their "disapprobation of elaborate wardrobes."[41] In a paper presented in 1880 at the Congress of the Association for the Advancement of Women, Professor Maria Mitchell of Vassar College complained that the costs of a girl's wardrobe greatly increased the price of her education. She asked, "Why should not girls club together, board themselves in a wholesome and inexpensive way . . . and dress for almost nothing?"[42]

This question proved naive. Female professors and administrators educated in the 1870s found precious few role models after they graduated from college. Their desire for a productive intellectual life conflicted with the domestic ideal, and these early graduates felt alienated because of their education. Frustrated with the limitations of social expectations, many decided not to marry.

The students at the turn of the century had a different experience. Emerging opportunities in the workplace and a growing respect for educated women lessened the tensions. Girls who entered college in the 1890s remained pioneers without the stigma of being outsiders. They viewed their college years as a wonderful adventure before marriage and sought to balance a modern identity with traditional values.

Most students, therefore, had no interest in discarding the pleasures of dressing up for unattractive wholesome styles. Students experimented with unconventional clothing for certain events, but these styles did not replace their fashionable dress. A style-conscious Chicagoan, Florence Hubbard, class of 1898, complained that she found no fashionable role models at Wellesley. "The faculty here dress so little and they are not generally in the latest style. Even the president generally appears in about the same style of gown no matter what the season is."[43] On her frequent trips to Boston, Florence kept her eyes open for the latest styles. Her efforts did not go unnoticed. In a letter to her mother, she described her classmates' reactions to a new silk. "You should have heard the girls comments. I had it all day long from right and left and by night I was nearly ready for something desperate."[44]

Women who concentrated on intellectual pursuits at the expense of their appearance were the targets of jokes and satiric commentary. Unlike the popular "all-around girls" or the "swells" who enjoyed an active social life, "grinds" concerned themselves with books only. Their indifference to dress made them immediately recognizable. "Her collar was traditionally unhooked, her shoe untied, and her whole aspect denoting a careless desolation." Grinds were stereotyped as skinny, pale, fashion misfits, and most students agreed that they would "rather see than be one."[45]

Dressing right, however, had its costs. Many style-conscious women found themselves exhausted every fall with the labor of dressmaking done on the preceding summer vacation.[46] The financial costs depended on the girl. "The very poor girl will probably spend somewhat more than at home; the rich girl somewhat less."[47]

The shirtwaist, a staple item in a woman's college wardrobe, suited the collegian's life-style well. Worn under jackets during cold weather, the waists came out in full force in the warmer months. The blouse appeared in every possible variation. Women favored plain white cotton waists for sportswear; more decorative versions in silk fit the bill on dressier occasions. As an emerging symbol of the new woman, the ready-made shirtwaist complemented a student's active and varied life-style perfectly.

Tailored skirts, another component of the collegiate wardrobe, also suited women's life-styles. Typically made of dark, heavy wool or cotton, these simple skirts could be dressed up or down easily. Several changes of skirts and waists provided students with a mix-and-match wardrobe. The skirts also offered the advantage of easy care—a thorough brushing and a quick pressing restored the skirts' neat appearance.

Students at all-women colleges sometimes shortened hemlines for greater freedom of movement, often with the support of the administration. In her 1896 letter to parents of incoming freshmen, the president of Wellesley College described the official position on appropriate dress. "The entire apparel should be made... in every way comfortable. Dresses should be short enough for easy walking."[48] On public occasions, officials expected girls to dress more formally, but within the privacy of the institution they encouraged a more relaxed attitude. Administrators, unlike dress reformers, did not seek to revolutionize women's dress, nor did they elevate fashion to a feminist cause. Instead, college officials advocated modified styles, such as a shortened skirt or a looser corset, to accommodate students' activities.

For some students, these changes required a period of adjustment. After observing the fashions of her classmates, one Wellesley freshman decided that she, too, would take the plunge. In her instructions to her mother, she requested a style five inches shorter than her black everyday skirt. "A good many of the girls here wear short skirts on rainy days. . . . Some have them come above their shoe tops, but I think to the tops is short enough."[49]

Smith College students, c. 1897. Many college women found shirtwaists and shortened dark skirts most practical for everyday wear.

During cold and long New England winters, students dressed for warmth. They layered outerwear over woolen chemisettes, jersey gaiters, and heavy stockings. Wellesley student Louise Pierce, class of 1900, wrote home to request a chamois vest, insisting that she did not want "any old imitation thing." She also expressed a preference for a winter cape instead of a coat. "We don't have time to take off our things from one recitation to another. . . . We keep our hats on all the forenoon but . . . its too much work to take it [the coat] off everytime, but I can just drop the cape."[50]

Louise's correspondence also provides insight into a rarely mentioned topic—laundry. The wealthier students sent their clothes to a laundress; those on tighter budgets did the work themselves. Louise describes the "awfully nice" washing facilities at Wellesley in a letter to her parents dated April 24, 1897:

> There are four set tubs with hot and cold water, of course, and in one of them a steam pipe arrangement runs which heats the water to more than boiling pitch. . . . So when we get done washing, we just put the clothes in that place, turn on the steam and they boil away to beat the band. Then . . . we take them out and put them in a drying box arrangement. . . . There are several boards and 2 or 3 dozen irons on an ironing stove.[51]

Although students at single-sex colleges dressed for dinner and wore the latest fashions to formal events, they often relaxed the rules for everyday dressing in the privacy of their all-female environment. The most obvious break with tradition occurred in the evolution of the collegiate athletic costume.

From their beginnings, women's colleges valued their students' health. By adding a strict exercise regimen to the curriculum, educators assuaged the concern of the mid-nineteenth century that an intellectual life overly taxed the "delicate sex." The prospectus of the Vassar Female College stated that "good health is essential to the successful prosecution of study." It added that this was especially true for women because of the "peculiar delicacy of their physical organization."[52]

Initially, instructors concentrated on walking, calisthenics, and light gymnastics to "give energy to the intellect." The standard exercise costume consisted of a shortened dress over loose-fitting bloomers. By the turn of the century, most schools had some form of regulation gym suit consisting of a middy blouse, baggy wool bloomers, and black wool stockings. To ensure compliance, some women's colleges included patterns and sewing instructions in their freshman orientation packet. When Wellesley student Louise Pierce showed up for freshman gym class, the instructor told her that her sweater must go. In a letter home, Louise explained the teacher's reasoning. "She can't see if my arms are straight if they are covered with big sleeves." She instructed her mother to make a blouse with sleeves "perfectly plain" but "big enough for free movement."[53]

The general acceptance of bifurcated athletic costumes was possible only in the privacy of a cloistered educational setting. While college officials were promoting physical activity, the public was still debating the merits of exercise for women. The bloomers that collegians slipped on each day for gym class caused jeers of derision when worn by dress reformers in public. Acutely aware of popular opinion, most college women wore traditional long skirts when exercising in public areas. Yet within the protected community of women, students chose a less confining style of exercise dress. The early experiments with bloomer outfits paved the way for a wider acceptance of bifurcated athletic clothing for college and noncollege women.[54]

By the 1890s, basketball was the favored sport at women's colleges. Introduced at Smith College in 1892, basketball combined the benefits of exercise with the excitement of a team sport. Dismissing calisthenics as "too tame," undergraduates embraced this new sport with enthusiasm. Dressed in the regulation baggy wool bloomers and middy blouse, students went onto the court willingly and even eagerly.

Initially, women's basketball and men's basketball were virtually the same game. Soon, however, educators began to fear the dangers of competition and rough play, which threatened to undermine their students' femininity. To accommodate a woman's "special needs," they modified the sport. The new rules placed team spirit over individual accomplishment. In defending this decision, Senda Berenson, the director of physical education at Smith College, stated that "unless a game as exciting as basket ball is carefully guided by such rules as will eliminate roughness, the great desire to win and the excitement of the game will make our women do sadly unwomanly things."[55] The revised rules divided the court into three sections and limited each player to one section to curtail excessive periods of running. Students could dribble a ball only three times before passing, and snatching the ball away from an opponent was forbidden.

Students at all-women colleges relished the exhilarating pleasures of physical training. They exulted at the temporary release from the constraints of corsets and the demands of books and tests. Rather than complaining about the physical education requirement, many women sought additional opportunities to exercise. Basketball, tennis, golfing, rowing, and archery all drew enthusiasts.

The American bicycle craze of the 1890s swept college campuses. The public debates over appropriate cycling dress, however, went largely ignored in college circles. Women accustomed to gymnasium bloomers and short skirts quickly agreed on the necessity of a safe, practical costume. The preferred costume was a short skirt worn over matching bloomers, which provided both freedom of movement and a modest appearance for the collegians' off-campus cycling excursions. Group consensus, however, still had to withstand the test of the individual. Louise Pierce's first experience with a "regulation suit" of bloomers, gaiters, and short skirt came in her freshman year. Despite her professed enthusiasm for the outfit ("They're great, shant ever ride in any other kind"), Louise clearly had doubts about the skirt. "The skirt is all right, it's plenty short, it seems very short to me."[56]

Women at most coeducational schools had a different experience when it came to physical education. Many complained that the colleges allocated most resources to men's athletics at the expense of women's physical education. In addition, the students directed the school spirit that supported and encouraged women at single-sex institutions toward men's team sports at coeducational institutions. The accomplishments of the campus football hero dwarfed those of the female athlete.

Women delighted in amateur theatrics, and they felt that they should be able to dress the masculine parts. The women in these Wellesley College productions portray the opposite sex successfully. Top, A Scrap of Paper, *1900;* middle, Love's Labour Lost, *1891;* bottom, A Russian Honeymoon, *1899.*

Even when times were set aside for women to use the gymnasium or the tennis courts, coed women never enjoyed the privacy and freedom that existed on all-women campuses. The differences translated into less progressive attitudes toward athletic dress. The presence of men made coeds reluctant to romp across the field in voluminous bloomers or to engage in fierce contests. Men often served as instructors for women's gym classes at these institutions, which further increased the tension between function and propriety.

In the 1890s, Northwestern required physical education for women, and students could choose from a range of sports. Although certain activities and team sports had their supporters, women's athletics failed to spark campuswide enthusiasm. In 1903, the Northwestern newspaper reported on a new campus pastime: "Some of the . . . girls are organizing walking clubs. The aim is to be able to walk to Chicago or to Lake Forest."[57] That the newspaper deemed such news noteworthy provides a striking contrast to the vigorous physical contests that took place at all-women colleges. While Northwestern girls celebrated a six-mile walk, Bryn Mawr students hobbled into supper on crutches after a Field Day basketball game.[58]

Some Northwestern students expressed concern that the level of women's physical education on campus did not match that of their sisters at the eastern colleges. The women's edition of the Northwestern campus newspaper published articles exhorting women to become more involved in physical education. "A little time spent on the rings in the gymnasium or a little extra exertion on the tennis court would simply do wonders for some of our girls."[59]

The contrast between the private sphere of single-sex colleges and the public space of coeducational schools influenced another realm of students' extracurricular dress—theatrical costumes. In all-women casts before an audience of peers, students performed masculine roles, and they strongly believed that they should dress the male part. When Vassar authorities suggested that women performing men's roles wear a short skirt and coat, students voiced their protest in the 1896 *Vassarion.* Urging the actresses to "be not too tame," they expressed their desire "to show beauty her own feature, manliness his own image."[60] Women succeeded in appearing on stage in men's frock coats and trousers only when no men were present. When students overstepped these boundaries, college officials exerted their

Women students in the 1890s sought to balance a modern identity with traditional values, just as this turn-of-the-century graduate balances her academic dress with traditionally feminine clothing and hairstyle.

authority. After Bryn Mawr officials caught a student walking around campus in trousers, they issued a formal regulation requiring women to change into skirts after theatrical performances.[61]

A review of campus policies during the 1890s reveals few formal dress codes. Undergraduate life still bore the imprint of Victorian society—a climate that made open defiance of societal norms untenable. Raised within the conventions of modesty, propriety, and conformity, these college women continued to adhere to traditional gender values. Yet within the safety of tightly controlled, sex-segregated environments, women experimented with unconventional behaviors and appearance. These small acts of defiance opened the door for the next generation of collegians. By the 1910s and the 1920s, students asserted their independence and challenged college policies. Rejecting traditional standards of personal behavior, students seized upon dress as a potent expression of their rebellion.

NOTES

1. Barbara M. Solomon, *In the Company of Educated Women* (New Haven: Yale University Press, 1985), 100.
2. Helen Lefkowitz Horowitz, *Alma Mater: Design and Experience in the Women's Colleges from Their Beginnings to the 1930s* (New York: Alfred A. Knopf, 1984), 159–69.
3. Horowitz, *Alma Mater*, 5.
4. Lynn D. Gordon, *Gender and Higher Education in the Progressive Era* (New Haven: Yale University Press, 1990), 5.
5. Gordon, *Gender and Higher Education*, 46.
6. M. A. Frost and J. H. Caverno, "What It Costs to Send a Girl Through College," *Outlook*, May 7, 1898, 82.
7. Mary Isabel Coates, "Getting Vassared," *Delineator*, September 1912, 136.
8. "Girl Life at Chicago University," *Chicago Tribune*, October 6, 1895.
9. Diary of Demia Butler, March 20, 1893, Department of Special Collections, Joseph Regenstein Library, University of Chicago.
10. Gordon, *Gender and Higher Education*, 139.
11. Horowitz, *Alma Mater*, 169.
12. Coates, "Getting Vassared," 136.
13. "Day Boarders," *University of Chicago Weekly*, February 23, 1899.
14. Louise N. Pierce to her parents, September 22, 1896, Louise N. Pierce Correspondence, Wellesley College Archives.
15. Paula Fass, *The Damned and the Beautiful: American Youth in the 1920s* (New York: Oxford University Press, 1977), 145–46.
16. Allen Guttman, *Women's Sports: A History* (New York: Columbia University Press, 1991), 115.
17. Raymond MacDonald Alden, "Academic Ceremonial," *Independent*, November 4, 1909, 1076.
18. *The Northwestern*, April 14, 1893, 112.
19. Horowitz, *Alma Mater*, 172.
20. Mary Caroline Crawford, *The College Girl of America and the Institutions Which Make Her What She Is* (Boston: L. C. Page & Company, 1905), 14–15.
21. "When College Girls Make Merry," *Ladies Home Journal*, November 1909, 34.
22. Crawford, *The College Girl*, 121; Horowitz, *Alma Mater*, 172–73.
23. Transcript of pamphlet of "Wellesley College" prepared for World's Columbian Exposition, 1893, Wellesley College Archives.
24. Margaret Sherwood, "Undergraduate Life at Vassar," *Scribner's Magazine*, June 1898, 658.
25. Solomon, *In the Company of Educated Women*, 107.
26. Suzanne Wilcox, "The Conduct of College Girls," *Independent*, August 7, 1913, 321.
27. "Confessions of a Co-Ed," *Independent*, October 10, 1907, 871–74.
28. Gordon, *Gender and Higher Education*, 87–88.
29. Gordon, *Gender and Higher Education*, 105–6.
30. *The Northwestern*, October 30, 1902.
31. "When A Girl is at College," *Ladies Home Journal*, September 1909, 32.
32. Gordon, *Gender and Higher Education*, 152; Horowitz, *Alma Mater*, 288.
33. Solomon, *In the Company of Educated Women*, 100.
34. *The Northwestern*, November 6, 1902.
35. Diary of Demia Butler, January 1893 to March 1893, Department of Special Collections, Joseph Regenstein Library, University of Chicago.
36. Marion Talbot to her mother, January 15, 1893, Marion Talbot Papers, Department of Special Collections, Joseph Regenstein Library, University of Chicago.
37. Edwin E. Slosson, "University of Wisconsin," *Independent*, July 1, 1909, 19.
38. Myrtle Whitney to her mother and grandparents, December 7, 1890, Letters of Myrtle Whitney, Department of Archives and Special Collections, Northwestern University Library.
39. Edwin Slosson, "University of Illinois," *Independent*, September 2, 1909, 532.
40. Hedwig L. Loeb's English theme, March 20, 1900, Hedwig L. Loeb Student Papers, Department of Special Collections, Joseph Regenstein Library, University of Chicago.
41. Circular to Parents and Students, August 1, 1882, Wellesley College Archives.
42. Charles F. Thwing, "College Education of Women, II: Important Auxiliaries," *Outlook*, May 12, 1894, 829.
43. Florence Hubbard to her mother, n.d., Florence Hubbard Correspondence, Class of 1898, Wellesley College Archives.
44. Florence Hubbard to her mother, n.d., Florence Hubbard Correspondence, Class of 1898, Wellesley College Archives.
45. "Point of View," *Scribner's Magazine*, December 1917, 765–66.
46. Thwing, "College Education," 829.
47. Frost and Caverno, "What It Costs," 83.
48. President's Office, Circular, 1898, Wellesley College Archives.
49. Louise N. Pierce to her mother, October 2, 1896, Louise N. Pierce Correspondence, Wellesley College Archives.
50. Louise N. Pierce to her parents, October 25, 1896, Louise N. Pierce Correspondence, Wellesley College Archives.
51. Louise N. Pierce to her parents, April 24, 1897, Louise N. Pierce Correspondence, Wellesley College Archives.
52. *Prospectus of the Vassar Female College* (New York: Alvord, 1865), 3–4.
53. Louise N. Pierce to her mother, October 14, 1896, Louise N. Pierce Correspondence, Wellesley College Archives.
54. Barbara Schreier, "Sporting Wear," in *Men and Women: Dressing the Part*, eds. Claudia B. Kidwell and Valerie Steele (Washington, D.C.: Smithsonian Institution Press, 1989), 98–101.
55. Senda Berenson, *Basket Ball for Women* (New York: American Sports Publishing Co., 1901), 20.
56. Louise N. Pierce to her parents, October 25, 1896, Louise N. Pierce Correspondence, Wellesley College Archives.
57. "Women's Edition," *The Northwestern*, April 2, 1903.
58. M. Carey Thomas to Mary Garrett, May 3, 1899, M. Carey Thomas Papers, Bryn Mawr College Archives, cited in Horowitz, *Alma Mater*, 159.
59. "Women's Edition," *The Northwestern*, April 9, 1896.
60. Sherwood, "Undergraduate Life at Vassar," 655.
61. Bryn Mawr Self-Government Association, Extracts from Minutes, December 8, 1897, February 17, 1898, March 17, 1898, M. Carey Thomas Professional Papers: History, Bryn Mawr College Archives, cited in Horowitz, *Alma Mater*, 163.

Everybody's Doing It:
College Life in the 1920s

The social transformation of the 1920s left adults feeling confused, angry, and old. They concluded that the younger generation was dancing, drinking, and petting itself into a "Babylonian breakdown of civilization," and they felt powerless to stop it.[1] Parents no longer understood their kids, and the kids no longer cared.

By the 1910s, the transformation of American life had already begun to erode the social order. World War I shattered Americans' complacent assumptions about progress. An expanding job market for women and the increased momentum of the suffrage movement focused attention on women's rights. The automobile and other forms of urban transportation opened up new terrain to explore. And the rise of new forms of mass communication, particularly in the entertainment field, and the proliferation of enticing advertisements presented tantalizing alternatives to Victorian life-styles. College campuses also witnessed unrest. Students of the 1910s actively challenged the political views held by authorities, and some women brought a heightened feminist consciousness to campus. Other radicals engaged administrations in ongoing questions of war and peace.[2]

These changes sent shock waves through society. To adults, with one foot in the ordered world of the nineteenth century, the modern world looked chaotic; the young, however, saw only the possibilities of the new. For youths coming of age in the late 1910s and the 1920s, the world seemed ripe for reinterpretation.

The younger generation demanded the right to be heard, and college students were the most visible and vocal representatives of this group. By 1920, 8 percent of Americans between the ages of eighteen and twenty-one attended college, a figure that would double by 1940. This was the decade when going to college became normal for youths of the middle class.

In the public discourse that celebrated and condemned these "shock troops of the rebellion," undergraduates occupied center stage.[3] In the past, rebel groups had been few and fragmented across a spectrum of causes. By 1920, however, youths focused on social reform. These issues, highlighted by the national media, found widespread support both on and off campus. By virtue of their position in the cultural spotlight, undergraduates became trendsetters. Noncollege youths, who similarly struggled with authority without the advantages of distance from family and a campus community of peers, assimilated collegiate dress and attitudes into their life-styles.

Northwestern's 1927 Purple Parrot *(opposite) and George Washington University's* Cherry Tree *(below left and right) depict tensions between youth and age in the 1920s. Dressed in clothing and engaged in activities that shocked the older generation, youths openly defied their elders.*

Strengthened by these multiple voices and frustrated by the puritanical values of campus officials, students mounted their attack. The inevitable contest ensued. College officials, who had once shaped the patterns of campus life, now had to contend with overt dissent. With the eagerness and arrogance of the young, college men and women demanded the right to establish a new set of rules. Snubbing tradition and openly defying authority, undergraduates reveled in their new freedom. Through music, clothes, and dance, they deliberately separated themselves from their parents' world.

In their battles with authority, students asked who has the right to dictate behavior and who decides issues of morality. Bewildered, adults feared the worst—moral anarchy. But they were not listening. Students wanted to extend, not destroy, the boundaries of permissible behavior. While the older generation routinely condemned youthful rebellion on the grounds of immorality, students responded that the problem was one of interpretation, not intention. "You mistake something fine for something degrading because it is different from your way of thinking."[4] Locked together in an interdependent campus system, students and administrators negotiated a new code of standards. The process cemented the collegiate peer group as an agent of change.

As new conventions replaced old values, peer approval supplanted parental consent. A revolution in manners could be realized only if students acted collectively. The demands of the group, therefore, superceded individual wishes; pressure to conform saturated campus life. Students of the 1920s endorsed group, not individual, dissidence. Youth rebellion focused on the acts of smoking, dancing, drinking, and sex.

Women proclaimed their new freedom by smoking cigarettes. At first a shocking act, smoking for female students gradually became accepted. By the end of the decade, Northwestern coeds (above) could light up without risking expulsion, or even exciting comment.

Above, a cigarette advertisement from Northwestern's Purple Parrot *associates smoking with outdoor recreation for men and women.*

Most of the furor over smoking centered on women. By lighting a cigarette, a woman committed a defiant act. Before this time, only prostitutes and bohemians flaunted the "noxious weed" in public. But women of the 1920s dismissed tobacco's immoral connotations, asserting that they had as much right to smoke as men. "Why shouldn't a woman have a taste for cigarettes just as a man has?" asked one coed. She protested that "a woman can command just as much respect with a cigarette in her mouth as without."[5]

Women did not simply challenge traditional notions of femininity when they smoked—they broke campus regulations. And the penalty for such defiance could be severe. In 1927, Goucher College suspended four freshman women for smoking in their dormitories.[6] Other college officials claimed jurisdiction even beyond the campus. The dean at Rhode Island State College threatened: "Any girl I catch smoking anywhere and at any time will not be permitted to remain in college."[7]

Students refused to modify their behavior. Heady with the notion of establishing their own rules, undergraduates identified themselves as part of a national campus culture. Student newspapers reported on the smoking debate at other schools, and examples of willful defiance spread from campus to campus. Editorials carried on the crusade. Placing itself firmly on the side of women's personal rights, the *Daily Northwestern* claimed that an administrative injunction against smoking did not deter women; it only drove them off campus where they could "smoke in the open." The newspaper took the position that cigarette smoking did not reflect on the smoker's morality.[8] Students were not going to buckle. Through their words and actions, they made a mockery of adult condemnations. An observer at the University of Michigan noted that while "expulsion follows when a girl is caught smoking, . . . the vast majority of them do smoke—secretly, of course."[9]

IT'S A GREY LIFE IF YOU DON'T WEEK-END

NOTHING ODD ABOUT THIS

This 1927 depiction of Northwestern "weekending" celebrates everything adults feared and the younger generation revelled in (above). Flappers smoke as they snuggle or dance with sheiks, the phonograph plays jazz music, and a butler delivers a case of bootleg whiskey. Right, a flapper from the 1929 Illio *displays the cigarette and painted face that the older generation found immoral.*

Parents railed at the dances of the "jazz inebriates" of the 1920s and worried about the more literal inebriation made possible by a hip flask (above). Knowing the latest dance steps as well as the local bootlegger remained important social attributes for their sons and daughters. Opposite, a 1925 DePaulian depicts student dances.

Recognizing the futility of imposing yet another set of sanctions, college officials reluctantly changed their position. The president of Mount Holyoke College noted that attempts to control students' behavior only increased their desire to rebel. "College women smoke principally because they resent being ordered not to smoke."[10] In 1926, Barnard College's physician prepared a list of smoking rules for students, some of which were designed to prevent women from such "mistaken paths" as cigar or pipe smoking.[11] By the end of the decade, however, most campus officials accepted smoking as a woman's prerogative. Stripped of its immoral connotations, the cigarette symbolized women's new sense of freedom and equality.[12]

The same issues of self-governance framed the debate about dancing on campus. For youths in the 1920s, dancing was an integral part of almost every social occasion; to fit in, one had to know the latest steps. In 1928, sociologist Robert Angell conducted a study of University of Michigan students. He reported that dancing was the most popular student diversion.[13] At Northwestern, the administration attempted to stifle the craze by prohibiting midweek dances. Undeterred, students simply went to local hotels.

But more than the frequency of dances, college administrators worried about the forms of dancing favored by the young. The shimmy, the toddle, and the Charleston brought partners dangerously close, and the sinuous movements of these "jazz inebriates" seemed charged with eroticism.[14] When the *Daily Maroon* polled University of Chicago faculty about their views on toddling, Mrs. Goodspeed responded, "I wish I had not lived to see it." Frederic Thrasher, a professor in the sociology department, agreed. "It is too suggestive. . . . This dance comes from the lowest and worst cabarets and is not for university people."[15] At Ohio State, citizens railed against the impropriety of "the girl's right arm below the man's right arm or around his neck" and placed the blame squarely on women's shoulders. As guardians of respectability, women should monitor their partners' actions.[16]

Determined to save students from "the rendezvous of iniquity," administrators tried to ban jazz dancing from campus. In 1921, Oberlin College barred the shimmy, the toddle, and cheek-to-cheek dancing.[17] Most schools charged chaperons with the responsibility of censoring improper dancing.

For students, the issue was self-expression. They protested that their dances were wholesome fun, and they questioned the administration's role in dictating behavior. Eventually, however, students and campus officials compromised. Students omitted the most extreme forms of jazz dancing and settled on styles of music and dance that they and the administration could live with. Fearing that hired chaperons and floor managers would result in dances filled only with the "old-fashioned two-step and waltz," students at the University of Illinois decided to act as their own censors. "Undesirables" who refused to modify their dancing style received a warning slip in the mail from the student monitors. After two warnings, the offender was barred from all university dances.[18]

Students of the 1920s did not reject the "old-fashioned" steps completely. Waltzing dominated the University of Chicago's traditional Washington Promenade, and students managed to have a good time. Many school newspapers reported on the students' proper behavior at proms and formal dances. Many college administrators, in turn, modified their positions. Admitting that their punitive measures to ban modern dancing had failed and acknowledging students' success in monitoring their peers' actions, officials turned the regulation of dancing over to students.

The issue of drinking could not be resolved so easily. With Prohibition firmly in place (the Volstead Act was not repealed until 1933), students who imbibed committed an act that was both defiant and illegal. Administrators presented on-campus drinking as the action of an irresponsible minority. Surveys from the period, however, reveal that students drank far more than their noncollegiate peers. Two Yale students appearing before a special Senate committee confirmed this finding. They testified that not only was alcohol accessible to students who wanted to drink but that the student body, in general, was antagonistic to the Volstead Act.[19]

Male students drank more than women did, and fraternities often came under attack for promoting the use of alcohol. Women, however, increasingly joined men in drinking a cocktail or sharing a glass of bathtub gin. It is difficult to separate the dare from the deed since no precise numbers exist on the number of students who drank during this period. It would also be incorrect to interpret drinking as one more generational challenge since students' parents also drank. In their efforts "to update conventional forms of behavior," however, students believed that the decision to drink should be an individual choice, not a government edict.[20]

Students' new freedom included rapidly changing attitudes about sexuality. While changing mores infiltrated society slowly, college youths shrugged off the repressive dictates of Victorian morality and openly experimented with new patterns of sexual behavior. In addition, they took what had previously been private acts and made them part of the public discourse.[21] Laughing at the hushed tones and obscure allusions that Victorians used when discussing "spooning," undergraduates openly flaunted their sexuality. As William Sassaman wrote to his friend John Rise, a student at the University of Chicago, "Any normal girl likes a kiss and a hug as much as you do." [22]

"Any normal girl likes a kiss and a hug as much as you do," a male University of Chicago student advised his friend. A 1927 Purple Parrot, *below left, and 1926 syllabus, below right, gave Northwestern students the same message.*

One author, lamenting the new generation, described the response of Mary Doakes, a fictitious college flapper, to a bashful man who asked her to dance. "Instead of the mid-Victorian curtsy and a modulated 'That would be charming!' she flips her cigarette among the palms and cries: 'Sold to the gentleman with the blonde mustache.'"[23] A letter to the editor in the *Daily Illini* complained about the new men on campus who cared only about dating. The author asked what happened to the man of the past who delighted in spirited conversations and athletic contests. He was now paired off with a coed, nestled in automobiles and campus soda shops, "whispering weak flub-dub . . . stroking hands, killing time and trifling with affections."[24]

Although they did not condone premarital sex or promiscuity, college men and women maintained that normal dating included "a bit of lovin'." Unlike the Victorian era's tightly controlled courtship system where each action and gesture was proscribed, dating opened up a new world of physical intimacy for youths. In the 1890s, a male suitor called on a woman at her parents' home, where the couple entertained themselves with card playing or reading aloud. As the friendship progressed, they might attend parties and church socials, but always under a chaperon's watchful eye. Young people in the 1920s, however, sidestepped the obstacle of parental approval and enjoyed romantic and sexual flirtation with numerous partners.

Couples moved out of the parlor and into movie theaters, dance halls, and the back seats of automobiles. In the words of one observer, "The ease with which a couple can secure absolute privacy when in possession of a car and the spirit of reckless abandon which high speed and moonlight drives engender have combined to break down the traditional barriers between the sexes."[25] Because of its scarcity on campus and the excitement it offered, the automobile became *the* status symbol. Women envied the girl whose date announced his arrival with the honk of a horn.

Students again turned to their peers rather than to parents or college officials for direction. Sexual experimentation became a fundamental part of the campus culture as youths defined popularity as getting dates—lots of them. In their new role as arbiters of sexual mores, youths celebrated necking and petting as desirable and permissible.

Although men still selected their companions, sexual politics were changing due to women's new assertiveness. To play the vamp, a woman had to play the field, chalking up conquests like trophies. In a fictitious letter, a coed flaunted her popularity with men before a hometown friend. "Five of 'em have . . . insisted I wear their [fraternity] pins. I don't tell any of 'em about the others, cause I'd hate to hurt their feelings. So I wear all their pins—but I won't tell you where!"[26]

A student poll at Northwestern University on "date getting methods" revealed that women often rejected the passive role. One coed recommended hanging around the journalism lab, another liked to stand near the ROTC bulletin board, and a third favored a more direct approach: "I wink at 'em in class."[27] Women at the University of Chicago opened a dating bureau to assist in the "intricate and often mythic" process of finding a date. Women interested in dating "well-known campus men" could specify the type of man preferred on a questionnaire.[28] At the University of California, a group of women attacked the "man problem" by declaring their independence: members of two sororities instituted a "no escort league" in which women pledged to attend college events alone. They hoped that once their peers grew accustomed to the idea, they could take the initiative and select their own escorts.[29]

Access to an automobile left even the idea of a chaperon far behind and created a "spirit of reckless abandon." Below left, University of Illinois students show the reason for escaping to the countryside. Below right, a 1925 DePaulian *depicts a fashionable couple enjoying a drive.*

Men on campus complained that women rated an evening based on the amount of money their dates spent. Articles bemoaning the high costs of dating appeared in campus newspapers. According to one Northwestern student, modern rules stipulated that a woman's responsibility was to "provide a satisfactory number of evenings at home with a minimum amount of illumination." In return, the man agreed to "act as escort and to shovel out the sheckels."[30] This new system of value and exchange prompted a University of Chicago man to reminisce about the good old days when women enjoyed "taffy-pulling, sleigh-riding and walking to an old-fashioned dance" and did not desire parties that were "purse-breaking."[31]

If a man's value lay in what he could provide his date, a woman's importance was measured by her ability to attract men. She had to have a stylish look, a catchy line, and modern sexual mores. Men made it clear, in the slang of the times, that they wanted a "good party" (a girl who necked and petted) for "snuggle-pupping."[32] The *Daily Northwestern* de-scribed a system used by some fraternity men to rate their dates; after a date with a new girl, "he walks up to the chart, grabs the swinging pencil, concentrates, and then rates her for the benefit of his brothers who want some dope before they date anyone."[33]

Women's heightened interest in sexual attraction and the changing codes of femininity found expression in their college fashions. Coeds loosened their waistlines and raised their hemlines, much to the delight of the men on campus. At a time when "knees were gay," women showed them off with "matter-of-fact carelessness." "Roguishly rouged" and "boyishly bobbed," self-possessed and fashion-conscious coeds challenged existing notions of how proper women should dress. Predictably, adults threw up their hands in despair at this "new degeneration." One observer suggested that the new skirts "wouldn't make a self-respecting pen wiper."[34]

Above left, the abbreviated bathing dresses and silk hose of the "Kiss Me Dolls" of Northwestern's Women's Athletic Association in 1922 contrast dramatically with women's sportswear of the 1890s. Left, a 1925 "prom girl" from George Washington University displays marcelled hair, Cupid's-bow lips, a beauty spot, heavy-lidded eyes, and an off-the-shoulder gown, all of which give her an air of open sexuality.

The abbreviated skirts, so prevalent on college campuses, signified sexual promiscuity to adult advisers. Although the brevity of the skirts has been exaggerated, hemlines did rise—at first to the calf and later to above the knee. This fashion shocked the older generation, which had deliberated on the propriety of baring a woman's ankles. After years of being hidden under layers of skirts and petticoats and shrouded in heavy cotton and wool stockings, legs were visible and provocatively encased in lacy hose and sheer silk stockings. The classroom display of women's legs prompted one visitor to exclaim: "That front row! It looked like the hosiery window at a spring opening or the finale of a Vanities first act."[35]

Adults did not limit their criticisms to skirt lengths. In their eyes, students' closets overflowed with examples of "flippant naughtiness." Even so small a detail as unbuttoned galoshes, or arctics, triggered criticism. When fashion persuaded women to walk around campus with their galoshes unfastened, student newspapers poked fun at the open boots, suggesting that the flapper appellation originated with this fashion. According to a limerick published in Northwestern's 1921 yearbook:

> The reason they let 'em go flapping
> Must be for the purpose of trapping
> The wild wanton eye
> Of the chance passer-by—
> And I'll say it keeps him from napping![36]

The humor was lost on an Evanston, Illinois, judge, who found the flapping arctics "too deshabille" to be really modest. He suggested a city ordinance to require the buckling of galoshes.[37]

Cutting off a "woman's crowning glory" seemed almost sacrilegious to the older generation, but campus women delighted in their bobbed hair as a fashionable symbol of freedom. Yearbooks from the mid- to late twenties yield almost no photographs of women with long tresses. Boyish and seductive, the short hairstyles embodied a new youthful sophistication. Unlike most styles that evolve over time, bobbed hair changed a woman's look overnight. Adult perceptions, however, could not adjust that quickly; they complained that the short hair reflected badly on a woman's morality. In the past, propriety demanded that women control their coiffures with dozens of hairpins and combs. The informality of youths' free-swinging styles implied a rejection of Victorian respectability. Youths viewed it differently. They claimed that short hair was both practical and modern. Topped off by a cloche hat, the new short hairstyles accommodated their life-style perfectly.

College students did more than follow fashion—they set the trend. Favorite collegiate styles, such as raccoon coats, became popular with youths both on and off campus. In the case of 'coon coats, men and women agreed that bigger was better. At the University of Chicago, the residence halls committee determined that closets in a new dormitory would have to be large enough "to accommodate fur coats."[38]

The popular coed had a stylish look, a catchy line, and modern sexual mores. Although Alice Judd, depicted in a 1925 Illio, *looks demure to us today, her elders probably found her bobbed hair and short skirts distressing.*

Styles of clothing and behavior went in and out of fashion with alarming frequency. Keeping up with campus fads was essential to belonging because in this intensely peer-conscious environment, youths fastened on clothing as an indicator of a student's loyalty to the group. In an article describing the typical collegiate wardrobe budget, the *Ladies Home Journal* reassured prospective freshmen, "You are not overemphasizing the importance of clothes. . . . A freshman is necessarily judged by her appearance."[39]

Sororities and fraternities helped to create and confirm the notion of a student pecking order. While turn-of-the-century students grouped themselves according to class affiliation, 1920s undergraduates found their place on campus in fraternities and sororities. Through their intense and often ruthless system of peer selection, Greek-letter societies engaged students in an ongoing process of competition, placing a premium on tangible symbols of success, such as clothes, dates, and automobiles. The contained environments of fraternity and sorority houses also enabled peers to monitor a student's devotion and adherence to group norms.

Following the most recent vogue, whether it was a slicker, purple pajamas, or a mah-jongg coat, marked an individual as part of the student community. But this devotion to fashion required money, a competitive spirit, and an insider's knowledge of the campus. The *Daily Maroon* emphasized the importance of distinguishing oneself from "the hoi polloi and the drug clerks." Otherwise, "the four years would be wasted."[40]

Campus flappers were not alone in adopting an aggressive attitude about dress. College men also demonstrated an avid interest in clothing and appearance. In their attempts to meet the current standards of physical and sexual attractiveness, young men oiled their hair, sported raccoon coats, and wore knickers. Ridicule awaited the naive freshman who arrived on campus in his unsophisticated "Kampus Kut Klothes," ignorant of his peers' stylistic edicts.

Adopting the latest fashions did not instantly transform a woman into a flapper. The serious expression of this Stanford student belies the carefree ease of her bobbed hairstyle.

Above, a 1928 Illio *depicts the extent of the popularity of raccoon coats for men and women.*

Glorified through the movies and reinforced by magazines, novels, and advertisements, the college man was one of the most popular media images of the 1920s. Winning the girls with his flashy dancing, smooth conversation, and stylish clothing, he presented a dazzling picture of youth. Immediately recognizable as a trendsetter of dress and manners, this media image helped spread the attitudes of youths into the middle-class arena. Fully aware of this mass appeal, manufacturers and retailers of men's clothing exploited the collegiate ideal in their advertising copy. Labeling styles as "Varsity" suits, "Campus" fashions, or "University" coats proved to be an effective marketing tool.

In their effort to promote a collegiate look, mass communicators often created a caricature. A satiric story in *Vanity Fair* concluded that the popular image of the college man, wearing Oxford bags, a letter sweater, and a varsity hat existed only in the comic strips.[41] Certainly, college men wore heavy sweaters, identifying insignia, and full-cut trousers. But the media presented a false picture of universal faddishness, as with the Oxford bags, those trousers that measured at least twenty-two inches around at each hem and, when viewed from the rear, gave the "illusion of a departing elephant."[42]

A story published in *The Phoenix*, the University of Chicago's student magazine, underscored the importance of dressing the campus part while poking fun at the outsider's view of the bags' iconic powers. Unsophisticated and naive, freshman Sonny Axelrod arrived on campus. Sizing up the situation, his cousin Fritz explained the importance of a man's wardrobe: "In college they judge you by the width of your pants. . . . The Kappa Gammas, the most exclusive society there . . . never consider anyone whose trousers are not at least twenty-two inches." Eager to fit in, Sonny purchased a pair of twenty-four-inch "bags" and immediately found himself "dated up."[43]

Students lampooned the bags in yearbooks, magazines, and theatricals, but photographic evidence of students wearing them is scarce. In 1928, *Vanity Fair* conducted a survey of Ivy League students and found few bags on campus. The magazine concluded that the only wearers must be noncollege men, who in their desire to look collegiate parroted a glossy media image. "We think that the retail clothiers and haberdashers are largely responsible for a popularity gained under false pretenses."[44] A local merchant interviewed by the *Daily Northwestern* agreed. While confirming that Oxford bags were a great advertising sensation, he added that "the fact that a large eastern store sells the bags only on special order shows there is not enough demand for them."[45]

Oxford bags were identified as a collegiate style. Above left, a cartoon from the 1925 DePaulian *shows a student examining his new acquisition. Left, a theatrical version of the wide-legged trousers.*

ATHLETICS

Media undoubtedly exaggerated the popularity of certain styles, yet no one could deny that clothing identified the college man as someone special. The most reliable sources of which fashions were in or out are the students of the time. In letters, published fiction, and campus reports, they confirmed that many wardrobe items, such as raccoon coats, were universally worn in college circles.

Undergraduates made it clear that for a fad to succeed, it had to be sanctioned by the "smart set." When a University of Chicago student addressed the Interfraternity Council in 1921, suggesting knickers as a comfortable and economical alternative to trousers, he acknowledged that if fraternity men wore knickers, "the fashion would soon be taken up by all the men on the campus."[46]

Reports of the knickers craze appeared regularly in college newspapers throughout the twenties. Knickers made headlines. Readers of the *Daily Northwestern* and the *Daily Maroon* could find out how the style fared not only on their own campus but at other schools across the country. "Students at Harvard to Sport Golfing Togs on Campus Again This Year."[47] "The *Daily California* has predicted . . . a brilliant future for the 'plus four' type of knickers."[48]

Restricted to boys under the age of ten during the first half of the nineteenth century, knickers gained popularity as adult sport clothing by 1900. Still worn by young boys in the 1920s, knickers suggested the lingering pleasures of childhood. Dressed in plus fours and colorfully patterned socks and sweaters, students presented a striking contrast to the starched collars and formal suits of their fathers. While the latter costume anticipated the seriousness of work, the former suggested leisure and playfulness.

Men at some schools wore knickers primarily for golfing; other male collegians deemed knickers as appropriate garb for most casual events. Princeton students followed an idiosyncratic rule that allowed only juniors and seniors to wear knickers. After studying the wardrobe of Princeton men, *Vanity Fair* concluded, "You can always recognize a Princeton Man—usually in the nick of time."[49]

Some styles were more ephemeral. In 1926, the *Daily Northwestern* described a new "cord dance" at the University of California. Any man appearing in *clean* corduroy trousers gained entrance. (Women were instructed to wear sport clothing.) "The purpose of the affair was to induce the men to wash their cords, as some had not washed them since the beginning of school last fall." The article went on to explain that upperclassmen at the University of California and Stanford wore corduroys as a sign of class distinction. Equally distinctive was the cord's presentation—peer edict frowned on excessive cleanliness. The wearer's class loyalty was "judged by the amount of dirt" accumulated by the time of the dance.[50]

WHEN A MAN GOES TO COLLEGE

Wear the two button English peaked lapel suit or the 3 button coat, lapels rolled to second button (right)

Worn by young boys and later as sports clothing in the nineteenth century, knickers suggested the pleasures of leisure. The 1929 Northwestern Syllabus, opposite. The 1929 spring catalogue for Hart, Schaffner, & Marx promoted a more formal collegiate look (left).

Clothing customs also enabled students to identify each other's status in the class hierarchy. Freshmen were at a particular disadvantage. The "procedure is for the upper classmen to parade all university customs before the eyes of the freshman at once, blinding and making them ill at ease."[51] Originally combined with hazing rituals in the nineteenth century, these campus traditions targeted male students. By 1900, most campuses banned excessive displays of physical roughness. Women remained largely exempt from class rituals.

Although upperclassmen declared that freshmen were immediately recognizable by their too-new clothing and awkward demeanor, the freshman cap left no room for doubt. In its promotional materials, Northwestern University described the cap in terms of a student's sense of duty. Distributed to fifteen thousand midwestern high school students in 1921, the booklet *With Northwestern Men* underscored the "sacred" importance of a class hierarchy. "Tradition makes . . . every building, every spot on the campus sacred to Northwestern men. . . . It dictates that all Freshmen shall wear the green cap with the purple button."[52]

Perhaps recognizing that some students might be unmoved by this high-minded appeal, the *Daily Maroon* chose a more direct approach: "Unless you are a Jack Dempsey or a capable swimmer we would advise you to fall in line."[53] While freshmen suffered the indignities of being forced to wear identifying insignia, seniors reaped the benefits of a tightly controlled class structure. On most campuses, certain styles were designated for seniors only. These rules had no exceptions.

In 1926, Northwestern men searched for a new sartorial sign for seniors. They rejected the initial choice of blazers in the school colors of purple and white because the coats proved too expensive. (They ranged in price from seven to twenty dollars.) Several weeks later, the *Daily Northwestern* announced that canes were the new fashion among seniors. At the price of one dollar, canes were accessible to all.[54]

Unlike Northwestern men who adapted the accessory of an aristocrat, Princeton seniors usurped a functional style of the workingman for their mark of distinction: white denim painters' overalls and jackets. The proud wearer of a "beer suit" often had an illustration "depicting some incident of college interest" stenciled on the back of the jacket. As a result, the suits were never laundered, which was all too evident by commencement.[55]

In the 1920s, the college flapper and her flamboyant beau became the symbol of freedom for a generation. They created a subculture of rebellious contemporaries who gave power to the group rather than to the individual. Removed from the watchful eyes of parents and chaperons, striving to win peer approval, undergraduates advanced a new code of morals, beliefs, and behavior. In the words of one fictitious coed: "Don't I make you jealous with all my good times? Home was never like this!"[56]

A 1923 Yale Record *(left) pokes fun at the many varieties of freshmen arriving on campus; a cartoon from a 1926* Purple Parrot *(opposite) shows that the addition of a green beanie distinguished any freshman.*

NOTES

1. Christian Gauss, "The New Morality in the Colleges," *Scribner's Monthly*, November 1931, 526.
2. Helen Lefkowitz Horowitz, *Campus Life* (Chicago: University of Chicago Press, 1987), 151.
3. Frederick Lewis Allen, *Only Yesterday: An Informal History of the 1920s* (New York, 1931; Perennial Library ed., 1964), 73.
4. *Ohio State Lantern*, February 3, 1925, cited in Paula Fass, *The Damned and the Beautiful: American Youth in the 1920s* (New York: Oxford University Press, 1977), 285–86.
5. Fass, *The Damned and the Beautiful*, 297–98.
6. "Frosh Women Smokers Are Suspended in East," *Daily Northwestern*, February 24, 1927, 1.
7. Fass, *The Damned and the Beautiful*, 285–86.
8. "Defending the Right to Smoke," *Daily Northwestern*, March 3, 1927, 1.
9. G. D. Eaton, "The Higher Learning in America," *Smart Set*, March 1922, 74.
10. "Coed Smoking is Due to Its Being Banned," *Daily Northwestern*, December 16, 1925, 3.
11. "Barnard Adopts Smoking Rules," *Daily Northwestern*, January 22, 1926.
12. Fass, *The Damned and the Beautiful*, 300.
13. Robert Angell, *The Campus* (New York: D. Applegate & Company, 1928), 165.
14. Fass, *The Damned and the Beautiful*, 302.
15. "Campus Stirred by Toddle Talk; Faculty Gives Views," *Daily Maroon*, January 21, 1921.
16. "Students at Ohio State Take Steps Against Accusations of Improper Dancing," *Daily Illini*, February 18, 1920.
17. "Oberlin Bans Toddle and Cheek-to-Cheek," *Daily Northwestern*, March 23, 1921.
18. "Start War on Shimmying as Dance Reform," *Daily Illini*, October 13, 1920.
19. Lawrence F. Abbot, "College Thinking About College Drinking," *Outlook*, May 5, 1926, 16–18.
20. Fass, *The Damned and the Beautiful*, 323.
21. Beth Bailey, *From Front Porch to Back Seat: Courtship in Twentieth-Century America* (Baltimore: Johns Hopkins University Press, 1988), 78–80.
22. William Sassaman to John Rise, December 26, 1919, John Manfred Rise, Letters and Memorabilia, Department of Special Collections, Joseph Regenstein Library, University of Chicago.
23. O. O. McIntyre, "Are Collegiate Flappers a Flop?" in *The College Years*, ed. A. C. Spectorsky (New York: Hawthorn Books, 1958), 472.
24. "Illini Degeneration," *Daily Illini*, May 14, 1923.
25. Angell, *The Campus*, 167–68.
26. "Letter From a Co-ed," *The Phoenix*, October 1925, 14.
27. "Aha! Campus Date Mongers Reveal Secrets of the Art," *Daily Northwestern*, May 17, 1923.
28. "Special Bureau is Suggested to Cope with Date Problem," *Daily Maroon*, December 7, 1921; "Date Exchange Opens; 20 Women, 73 Men Sign," *Daily Maroon*, December 8, 1921.
29. "University of California Girls Campaign for Feminine Freedom," *Daily Northwestern*, April 10, 1926.
30. "Cupid Laughs at Ban on Campus Marriages," *Daily Northwestern*, October 17, 1925.
31. "Present High Cost of Co-Education is Alarming say Men," *Daily Maroon*, December 2, 1921.
32. "College Slang a Language All Its Own," *Literary Digest*, March 14, 1925, 65.
33. "Fraternities Have Social Registers to Record Dates," *Daily Northwestern*, May 17, 1923.
34. Bernard de Voto, "The Coeds Were Real—The Boys Were Shadows," reprinted in *The College Years*, ed. A. C. Spectorsky (New York: Hawthorn Books, 1958), 494; McIntyre, "Are Collegiate Flappers a Flop?" 472.
35. Bernard de Voto, "The Co-ed: The Hope of Liberal Education," *Harper's Magazine*, September 1927, 452.
36. "The Flappers," *Northwestern Syllabus*, 1921, 293.
37. "Co-eds Should Button Arctics, Says Judge," *Daily Northwestern*, January 5, 1921.
38. Minutes, Residence Halls Projects, February 14, 1929, Department of Special Collections, Joseph Regenstein Library, University of Chicago.
39. Margaret Matlack, "A Clothes Budget for the College Girl," *Ladies Home Journal*, August 1924, 63.
40. "Doing the Raccoon," *Daily Maroon*, February 5, 1929.
41. Corey Ford, "Ready-Made College Types," *Vanity Fair*, September 1926, 72.
42. "What the College Man Really Wears," *Vanity Fair*, September 1926, 92.
43. Andrew Johnson, "The Extraordinary Adventures of Sonny Axelrod," *The Phoenix*, January 1928, 15.
44. "What the College Man Really Wears," 92.
45. "Oxford Bags Doomed, Knickers To Be the Thing," *Daily Northwestern*, September 25, 1926.
46. "Knickers May Become Standard Garb for Men," *Daily Maroon*, November 2, 1921.
47. "Students at Harvard to Sport Golfing Togs on Campus Again This Year," *Daily Maroon*, September 23, 1920.
48. "Oxford Bags Doomed, Knickers to Be the Thing."
49. Ford, "Ready-Made College Types," 72.
50. "Corduroy Trousers Worn to Dances in Fad at California," *Daily Northwestern*, April 15, 1926.
51. "Save the Freshmen," *Daily Northwestern*, October 6, 1925.
52. "Spirit Makes Northwestern Great, Says New Booklet," *Daily Northwestern*, May 30, 1924.
53. "Radical Style Change in Frosh Headgear is Planned Today," *Daily Maroon*, October 12, 1920.
54. "Toting Canes New Fashion Among Seniors," *Daily Northwestern*, March 12, 1926.
55. "What the College Man Really Wears," 94.
56. "Letter from a Co-ed, No. 2," *The Phoenix*, November 1925, 14.

Students of the twenties might have sought a string of conquests, but students of the forties looked for stability and tended to pair off, like this amorous couple from Northwestern University.

Going for the Mrs. Degree: College Life in the 1940s

Events of the 1930s shattered the high-spirited rebellion and self-involved experimentation of 1920s college youths. The flappers' antics seemed frivolous to 1930s undergraduates trying to confront the problems of their decade. In the wake of the stock market crash, going to college became a rare privilege and unthinkable for most families. The depression undermined the promise of higher education; a college degree meant little in the unstable job market. And the growing threat of war awakened students from their political apathy. Collegiate social consciousness took a decided turn to the left as students rallied around the cause of peace. When students organized a peace strike in 1936, half a million undergraduates participated.[1]

The outbreak of World War II ended campus cries for pacifism and brought about a renewed seriousness about studies and a reconsideration of values. Challenged by the immediacy of war, students rallied together in a spirit of patriotism. Many delayed or interrupted their education to join the troops; those who remained on campus dedicated themselves to supporting the cause. Students understood that there was something beyond the ivy-covered walls that was bigger than their four-year plan.[2]

With over fifteen million men serving in the military, the social dimensions of college life changed dramatically. Women had to adjust their expectations of four years of dating followed by marriage; rather than deferring their dreams, many rushed into a "marriage marathon."[3] As they watched their classmates drop out of school to marry or become campus-furlough brides, the remaining coeds wondered if their turn would ever come. Unlike the students of the 1920s who delighted in the notion of dating with "no strings attached," undergraduates of the 1940s yearned for commitment.

Above, peace strikes of the mid-1930s disappeared with the beginning of World War II. Below, Mundelein College women prepare for the worst in first aid courses, and University of Chicago coeds waiting to audition as chorus girls for a war benefit use spare moments to knit— perhaps bundles for Britain or socks for soldiers.

Above, Bethune-Cookman home-economics students prepare a victory dinner. Below, University of New Hampshire women participate in an ROTC-like program created for them. With the onset of the war, women's physical education became more strenuous.

Never losing sight of the reasons for the hard times, women threw themselves into war-related service work. Wellesley and Smith women organized "peeling parties" to remove the tinfoil from cigarette packages, and home-economics students at the University of North Carolina received college credit for testing recipes for army cookbooks. Women drove ambulances, practiced first aid, and rolled bandages. They sold war bonds, organized blood banks, and wrote V-mail. And on every campus they knit furiously to send bundles to Britain.[4]

Coeds at the University of New Hampshire organized a physical training course, the first in the country, modeled after the ROTC program, to prepare themselves for military service. In an unofficial uniform of light-blue shorts and blouses, the girls hiked, exercised, and tackled the "rigorous man-sized obstacle course." Beginning in the winter of 1943, the school required freshmen, sophomores, and juniors to spend three hours every week making themselves fit. An upcoming military ball, however, provided a break in the routine. According to *Life* magazine, it became necessary to stop all exercises for a few days because "the girls were too stiff to dance."[5]

The war temporarily reshaped professional opportunities for women. As an increasing number of men exchanged collegiate clothes for khaki uniforms, women found themselves in the campus majority for the first time. While some college officials insisted that women could best preserve the American and democratic spirit by enrolling in courses that supported traditional values, such as those in home economics, other schools broke through gender barriers.[6] Acknowledging both the scarcity of men and the escalating wartime demands for highly trained professionals, some administrators encouraged women to enter fields that had previously been dominated by men. Female enrollment in such courses as meteorology and engineering swelled. In 1943, an article in the *New York Times Magazine* reported that "almost weekly students receive letters from chemical plants or scientific laboratories . . . urging girls to enter those fields."[7] Barnard College offered its students short-term, extracurricular instruction in map making, mechanical draftsmanship, and motor transport.

At the end of the war, educators and students reconsidered these advances. Many women relinquished their positions to make room for the millions of young men returning home. Embracing the peacetime priority of a return to normalcy, colleges rekindled the notion of a woman's place. Tradition dictated that a woman should be in the home, not in the factory or laboratory. A number of women activists tried to sustain the advances women achieved during the war; their successes, although tangible, were limited. Public opinion and personal interests overpowered the faint voices of feminism.

The postwar years witnessed another upheaval in the demographics of college enrollments. With the passage of the Servicemen's Readjustment Act in 1944, more men could attend college than ever before. Returning veterans took advantage of the generous college benefits attached to the GI Bill, and they came to campuses in unprecedented numbers. In 1946, more than one million GIs enrolled in college, and between 1946 and 1948 veterans composed almost one-half of all college students.[8] But more than numbers made this sudden influx of servicemen so revolutionary. College veterans were older, and many were married and had children. The GI Bill of Rights challenged the elitist structure of higher education, permanently changing expectations of who had the right to go to college.[9]

In the wake of these events, students struggled to salvage a college experience. Students sought something to hold on to, and they clung to the stability of the group for reassurance. The group, in turn, mirrored the conventions of society. Fitting in had never been more important.

On many campuses, students turned to sororities and fraternities as the ultimate college authority. These groups set absolute standards and created elaborate systems of rules and rituals. Membership in this select group demanded loyalty to the chapter, both locally and nationally, and strict adherence to the morals and mores of the house. In return, a student was welcomed into "one of the nerve centers of university life."[10] But the very nature of these closed membership organizations bred competition, ranking individuals and groups according to popularity and status.

One author, speaking out against sororities in an article for *Mademoiselle*, railed against the system for its complete submersion of the individual. In her opinion, sisters "talk alike, play bridge alike, even try to force the sisters to vote alike at campus elections."[11] Critics also attacked the social exclusiveness of Greek-letter societies and the stigma attached to the students who failed to pass muster. In a profile of rush week at the University of Colorado, *Life* observed that, at the end of the week, "the freshman will be accepted or rejected as a member of a sorority, a fact which will influence her social life and her happiness all through college."[12] Indeed, on many college campuses, sororities and fraternities dominated a student's extracurricular experiences.

Veterans flooded onto campuses after the war. Many, like the University of Chicago law student above, brought their families to live in quickly erected married students' housing. If veterans were single when they returned to campus, they might not remain so long. Right, a 1947 couple at Northwestern becomes officially pinned as an entire sorority witnesses.

Although rushing took place in the fall, the evaluation process often started the summer before when sororities formed "caravans" to interview prospective initiates. Hopeful freshmen monitored every action since even the slightest social slip could prove grounds for blackballing. A 1939 article in *Mademoiselle* left no doubt as to how carefully a girl would be scrutinized: "The sisters watch your dress (which should be neat but not gaudy), your conversation (delightful but not dominating), your manners (courteous, not curt), and your friends (birds of a feather)."[13] And this was just the beginning. Sororities examined a rushee's social position, her "popularity quotient," her religious and ethnic background, and whether or not she would be a "good 'dater.' "[14]

Because the war created a temporary shortage of men on college campuses, dating became fiercely competitive. In 1947, the *Science News Letter* ran an article blaming a myriad of social, emotional, and health problems found among college women on the scarcity of men. The author found that even after the end of the war, college girls suffered from feelings of depression and insecurity. The reason? Fewer social activities, fewer available boys, and the "fear lest she miss her chance to get married."[15]

Campuses housing military training camps retained a larger male population during the war than other colleges. Opposite, well-dressed Northwestern coeds meet military men on the library steps, 1945. Above, because schools enforced strict visitation hours, women had residence halls to themselves on weeknights.

The statistics were sobering. *Newsweek* cited that during the war women composed up to 90 percent of the enrollment in many universities and colleges.[16] Coeds at the University of Chicago and Northwestern University faced better odds because these campuses served as military training bases for thousands of servicemen. But even this infusion of men failed to stabilize the situation. Military men had different priorities than undergraduates, and they often refused to play the college game.[17] Frustration mounted when the shortage of available men continued after the war. Many of the returning GIs were already married, and perhaps more alarmingly, a vocal faction of single veterans rejected the coed as a desirable companion. Older and sobered by the war, they protested that they wanted women, not girls interested in teasing games of courtship. Women had to face the reality that "one girl in every seven will have to live alone, whether she likes it or not."[18]

What was a girl to do? One commentator lamented that a growing number of girls, fearful of becoming "old hags" at twenty-six, dated "almost anything that grows whiskers—or peach fuzz." They lowered their standards because "many would rather have a drip than no man at all."[19] Others tried to gain the competitive edge by waging strategic battles. Magazine articles claimed that women intent on "hooking a man" had to be willing to change their hair, their dress, and even their personality. The *Ladies Home Journal* offered college girls a "personality do-over plan" with the promise that "if you start now, you can name your own prize: the right guy saying, 'What are you doing New Year's?' "[20]

Seventeen schooled girls in the art of conversation. The goal was to get the boy to talk about himself. To get a girl started, the magazine offered sample conversational gambits:

> You: You have hands like a doctor's. Did anybody ever tell you that?
> Joe: No—yes—whaddya mean?
> You: Well, they look strong and—well, sort of efficient.

How could Joe resist? In case the reader missed the point, the magazine issued a final warning: "When you see a boy opening his mouth, shut yours immediately."[21]

When sociologist Mirra Komarovsky conducted a survey of sex roles among college women in 1946, she discovered that a disturbing percentage of her subjects felt the need to "play dumb" with men. One girl revealed a favorite technique. When corresponding with her boyfriend, she deliberately misspelled long words because he seemed to "get a great kick out of it." Another expressed her confusion over the mixed messages she received from home. While her father expected her to get straight As, her mother pleaded, "Please don't become so deep that no man will be good enough for you."[22]

If the immediate challenge was getting a date, the goal for many women was marriage. Postwar society celebrated women's roles as mothers and wives, and the presence of married veterans on campuses only increased the coeds' interest in matrimony. Peer pressure and public sentiment encouraged women to return to their "rightful place" in the home.[23] And with newly installed prefab housing available to married students, women's rightful place could be as close as the edge of campus. As more and more undergraduate women embraced the domestic ideal, they came to view college as a "marriage market."[24]

For many women, a diamond ring on the third finger defined a successful college education. Women and men felt no uneasiness that marriage signaled the end of youth, catapulting the couple into adulthood; the war had already done that. When the *Daily Northwestern* polled coeds on their motives for going to college, the number one answer was men. College curricula often supported the goals of these "pre-weds." Students enrolled in family life classes and home-economics courses to gain practical skills that would make them better wives and mothers. The University of Nevada offered a marriage course "for those who expect to marry soon after graduation." To register for Stephen College's cooking class, a girl had to "be a senior, engaged, [and] interested in cooking for two or more."[25]

Above, a pin from the right sorority or fraternity held the promise of social success. Top to bottom: Kappa Alpha Theta sorority, Pi Beta Phi sorority, and Sigma Chi fraternity. Tips on social success could also be gleaned from magazines. Middle, a 1942 North Park coed studies Charm *during her bath. The goal for men and women was to become part of a happy couple (right).*

Sororities reinforced the importance of going for the "Mrs. degree." The Alpha Epsilon Phi chapter at Northwestern publicly stated the group's goal in their 1949 newsletter: "Husbands for all A E Phi seniors so they will not graduate a disgrace to their sorority."[26] Sororities celebrated with elaborate rituals the success of the sister who had caught her man. At the University of Southern California, Delta Delta Delta coeds hosted a party every spring to honor all engaged seniors. A loudspeaker broadcast the couples' names as the brides-to-be stepped through a pansy ring, one by one.[27]

Getting pinned was often the first step toward the altar, and Greek-letter societies publicly celebrated the event. Sorority sisters witnessed this declaration of a man's intention while his fraternity brothers serenaded the couple in the background. When Newton Minow pinned his sweetheart Jo Baskin at Northwestern in 1946, their out-of-town friends sent telegrams. "Congratulations. You're one step closer to that duplex in Milwaukee."[28]

The intense romantic and sexual competition underscored the importance of women's appearance; you had to lure a man before you could catch him. Certainly, the right clothes did not guarantee success, but the wrong clothes marked one as an outsider. An adviser for *Seventeen* urged girls to curb any instinct they might have to look different. She suggested they go to college "looking as conventionally attractive as possible . . . as Susan-the-newcomer, be a follower, a wearer of the tried-and-true, the accepted." She predicted that girls who ignored her advice would "pay for it."[29]

One writer for the *New York Times Magazine* attributed this will to conform to youthful insecurity and a college environment that turned classmates into rivals. She claimed that behaving and dressing similarly seemed to give college women "confidence and strength."[30] Authors of a study of home-economics students concluded that "a strong desire exists in each girl to conform to her group's standards."[31]

Sweatshirts, saddle shoes, and dungarees (left) sufficed for an evening in the dorm, but even a casual date required coeds to carefully prepare makeup, hair, and dress (middle). A University of Southern California Tri-Delt (right) dressed elegantly for the announcement of her engagement at the "Pansy Breakfast," 1945.

Even undergraduates whose behavior and dress challenged mainstream values were classified and labeled. Contemporary observers noticed that these rebels found support and like-minded women at certain colleges. One *Mademoiselle* article identified five categories of female students: academic, social, artistic, rah-rah, and political. Describing the artistic girl as one who "costumes herself in stark off colors, [and] binds her feet back to earth in thong sandals," the author commented that this type appeared "most often at Black Mountain, Bennington, and Sarah Lawrence." The University of Chicago and New York University tended to attract the political type who "takes her coffee black (no sugar) in the proletarian diners where she argues Aragon and Trilling, Marx and Reich with others of her kind." You were likely to find her late at night, in her flannel bathrobe, "despairing of saving the world in spite of itself."[32]

The concept of a college wardrobe was firmly entrenched by 1940. Usually purchased the summer before a girl entered college and designed to help a coed "click" with the group, these coordinated outfits held the promise of a new life. One woman remembers how her mother invited her friends over to view her sister's college wardrobe: "She laid out all of the new clothes on the bed. . . . It was like a bride's mother showing off her daughter's trousseau."[33]

Entering freshmen found plenty of assistance in choosing the right campus looks. Fashion magazines, such as *Mademoiselle* and *Glamour*, devoted their August issues to collegiate dress. And the bobby-socks brigade had another choice when *Seventeen* was launched in 1944.[34] Bulging with ads and advice, these campus-oriented issues became the Bible for most college-bound women.[35] "My friends and I used to pore over the pages of *Mademoiselle* fantasizing about an unlimited budget and a trunkful of cashmere sweaters," reminisced a 1946 graduate of Vassar.[36]

Fashion magazines acknowledged college students as important arbiters of taste. In an interesting reversal of the clothing feuds mothers waged with their daughters in the 1920s, daughters in the 1940s sometimes dictated standards to their mothers. *Good Housekeeping* warned the anxious mother that a daughter "views you with a supercritical eye" and "wants you to outshine all other mothers." Kittenish mothers who tried to dress like their daughters were particularly scorned. The formula for success? Tailored clothing.[37]

While providing their readership with the basics of a collegiate wardrobe, fashion magazines urged their readers to seek out students attending their school for specific fashion advice.[38] One woman, having sought such advice, worked the summer before her freshman year, saved $455, and specified to her mother's dressmaker exactly what she wanted. "I went off to school knowing that I would fit in."[39]

Most major department stores also provided help. College shops, open all year or just for the summer months, employed college girls. Founded on the principle that "it takes one college girl to sell another," these shops hired sophomores and juniors to advise their peers in wardrobe planning. "The store wants to use the girls' names to attract their friends, and the college names to mark the store's clothes as right for those colleges."[40]

Students on campus could read about the latest fashion dos and don'ts in their campus newspapers and magazines. Reporters covered local as well as national trends, often turning a fashion spotlight on the school's most popular coeds. In 1942, Northwestern's *Purple Parrot* noted that "Nancy Spitzi . . . possesses THE date dress, purple wool with velveteen paneling down the front."[41] A reporter for the University of Chicago's *Pulse* magazine instructed readers to look to other students for inventive fashion solutions. *Pulse* singled out Cathy Elmes as the girl "who takes a hint from *Mademoiselle* and ties bows around her neck, slanted slightly to one side, and peeking above the jacket of her suit."[42]

Every fall, college girls returned to campus in their sweaters and skirts. Pleated or gored tweed skirts that fell to just below the knee were essential, but Shetland sweaters (or cashmere for the lucky) formed the backbone of women's collegiate wardrobes. Sweaters appeared in every imaginable style, including cardigan, cable-knit, pullover, crewneck, V neck, and sweater sets. Students dressed them up with a string of pearls, layered them over blouses and dickies, and, in faddish moments, wore their cardigans buttoned up the back. With oversized sweaters, the sleeves were pushed up to the elbow.

For more than a decade, saddle shoes identified a generation of students. Unlike students' coordinated daytime outfits and sophisticated evening wear that echoed the taste of their parents, saddle shoes remained the prerogative of youth. Saddle shoes expressed an identification with youth rather than an explosion of group dissidence. While mothers exhorted children to polish their shoes more frequently, parents responded to the fashion of scuffed saddle shoes with more amusement than anger.

In 1941, *Good Housekeeping* described the loyalty girls felt for the saddle shoe. "Limp, dejected, dirty though it may be, thousands of college girls cling to it fiercely, love it dearly."[43] First worn by college students, these brown-and-white oxfords were subsequently adopted by high school students. Campus protocol dictated thick white bobby socks, never knee socks, as the appropriate accessory. Students also understood that the shoes should never look new. In the words of one Vassar woman, "There is . . . a certain eclat attached to dirty footwear."[44]

Both mothers and daughters favored man-tailored clothing during the 1940s (opposite). Above, Smith students combine tailored shirts and jackets with casual dungarees and shorts. Right, scuffed saddle shoes were worn with almost any outfit, as shown by this University of Chicago student (right).

In addition to the ubiquitous saddle shoe, women wore moccasins, espadrilles, and loafers. Admirers of the "ballet russe" look favored flat leather skimmers. Rubber boots and fur-lined "stadium boots" kept feet warm in winter. For dressier events, women slipped into heels and silk stockings carefully set aside for special occasions.

College women agreed about the basic elements of their campus wardrobe; however, they split into factions over pants. Although the debate lacked the passion that characterized the sartorial clashes of the twenties, it injected a jarring note of dissension into this sea of conformity. Attitudes varied from campus to campus. When *American Magazine* polled undergraduates on whether girls should be allowed to wear shorts and slacks on campus, nearly half of the respondents answered *no*.[45] An article published in *Hygeia* tried to reassure parents that these styles were an understandable and harmless response to the bewildering adjustment to college life. "What to an adult eye is classified as almost a slovenly appearance, becomes a badge of group superiority."[46]

In 1941, *Mademoiselle* highlighted the popular styles at fourteen schools. Vassar students wore slacks during the day but declared them taboo at dinner. University of Michigan women described the dominant campus look as "conservative and impeccable" and discouraged prospective students from bringing any slacks for campus wear.[47] In another survey, Radcliffe students ruled out shorts, slacks, and blue jeans entirely.[48] When residents of Northwestern's Willard Hall published a guide for freshmen entering the university in 1948, they spelled out the dormitory's policy on blue jeans. "Dungarees are O.K. at breakfast and lunch, but never dinner."[49] The University of Chicago left the decision to the individual. For many of these urban coeds, pants fulfilled both a psychological and a physical function: they conveyed a spirit of intellectual bohemianism while offering warmth and protection from the icy winter winds.

With these Chicago coeds, however, neatly tailored slacks often gave way to frayed and faded blue jeans rolled up to the knees. The widespread popularity of women's dungarees at that campus sparked a heated debate in the *Daily Maroon*. In a letter signed "Disappointed Dan," a member of the Army Specialized Training Program accused the coeds of being sloppy and socially immature. After visiting various campuses across the country for his military training, Dan found the sight of Chicago women with "blue jeans rolled up to the hips and sweaters drooping down to meet them" disappointing and dispiriting.[50] A week later, the paper published this angry response:

The "dungy" on this campus is one of our important manifestations of real democracy. It levels the display of economic inequality stressed by the glamour college. . . . I don't know what you're here for, Dan, but we're here to improve our minds and become better citizens. And we'd rather spend our time pursuing that end than ironing that extra frill or baking under permanent-waving apparatus.[51]

A photograph of two Wellesley students dressed in men's shirts and well-worn dungarees appeared in *Life* in 1944, and it piqued the nation's interest. The *New York Times Magazine* took note of blue jeans as the new academic badge and tried to answer "Why College Girls Dress That Way." After interviewing students and analyzing the motivations and the meanings of their dress, one writer concluded that it boiled down to "the desire for comfort, the locale of the school, the absence of men, the war and last, but not least, an unashamed desire to be 'different.'"[52]

In their desire to be different, college women borrowed liberally from the male closet. They raided men's shops for raincoats, caps, trousers, sweaters, and shirts.[53] Insisting on the genuine article, college girls invested in right-buttoned jackets. Beginning in 1940, the trend first caught the interest of eastern women's colleges and then quickly spread west. According to the *New York Times*, men's clothiers targeted women as potential customers. Their advertising copy suggested "that a girl going to a really good school would be just about ostracized if she wasn't practically indistinguishable from a Princeton sophomore." The author dismissed the suggestion that the war created this sudden craving for masculine apparel. In her opinion, girls wore the clothes because they were novel and "becoming."[54]

The studied casualness of classroom and dormitory clothing provides a striking contrast to the formality of date dressing. Dungarees, although comfortable and youthful, were hardly date bait. Depending on the occasion, women changed into fitted suits, tailored crepe garments, or formal gowns. Fashion advisers and retailers promised that these styles transformed the "sloppy joe girl" into a sophisticated woman. A black velvet dance dress "iced with glistening rayon taffeta" from Carson Pirie Scott & Co. instantly transported the lucky wearer from "casual classroom cardigan to regal elegance." The demure student turned siren in a formal bouffant dress in black and "heaven blue."[55]

Dressing up involved more than a change of clothes; women's demeanor proved equally transmutable. A writer for the *New York Times* observed that "the Monday frumps in pigtails are unrecognizable as fashion plates on Saturday." She dubbed this phenomenon the beauty and the beast syndrome.[56] With a change of clothes, the all-around girl turned into the alluring belle, dressed to charm and disarm her date:

A formal date required a different look from day-to-day clothing; women often underwent an astonishing weekday-to-weekend metamorphosis. University of Chicago students enjoy the "Heavenly Dance" of 1947 (below left); a University of North Carolina coed displays her formal gown the same year (below right).

No one would ever believe that you can beat the boys at tennis—or that you lead the geometry class, hands down. From the moment a long, swooshy skirt settles around your ankles, you take on new poise and charm. You don't lope across the floor the way you might in dungarees. . . . Tonight you let your date open doors and fetch your supper.[57]

A Northwestern man was less pleased with the chameleon-like behavior of his dates. "During the week," he explained, "they're seen in saddle shoes and sweaters and they beam when you buy them a coke. On week-ends, however . . . on go the fake eyelashes and it takes dinner at the Drake to produce even a flicker."[58]

Peer standards of attractiveness also affected men. The BMOCs (big men on campus) endorsed certain fashions and expected campus newcomers to conform. A reporter for the University of Chicago's *Daily Maroon* offered college men advice: "Stay away from faddy things; stay away from the things mother made you wear in high school."[59] The fashionable menswear of the forties and the undergraduate styles differed only slightly. After all, fashion extremism and clothing statements of student rebellion were out of place at a time of national emergency. School was serious business, and many men accelerated their college program to join the fight. But college men did assemble a look that expressed the wearer's youthfulness and corollary freedom, however temporary it might be.

Manufacturers and retailers of men's clothing advanced the notion of a distinctive campus look by injecting college-oriented copy into their promotional campaigns. Rather than stressing the uniqueness of their products, advertisers underscored the widespread acceptance of the styles. Van Heusen proclaimed itself the "alma mater" of college men, Haggar claimed their slacks to be the "keenest on the campus!" and C. B. Shane Corporation promoted its Season Skipper model as "the coat with a college degree." Manhattan Shirts advertisements featured "an authentic college wardrobe" approved by their college style committee, while the manufacturers of Alligator raincoats held out the promise of success with college coeds. "Soggy classmen *try* to date her but the men who *win* wear ALLIGATOR!"

Collegiate men seeking a fashion textbook could find it in September issues of *Esquire* magazine. These back-to-school editions counseled men on the finer points of college dressing. While noting that "nearly all of the universities have some . . . individual fashion favorites," *Esquire* promoted a "basic campus wardrobe that would tag a man as summa cum fashion" anywhere.[60]

Clothes figuring?

Hart Schaffner & Marx Clothes

By the 1940s, men had long since rejected fads of the twenties, such as Oxford bags, knickers, and raccoon coats. Above, students arrived at school with trunks full of classic, tailored clothing, such as that featured in the Hart, Schaffner, & Marx advertisement of 1946 (left).

Following the pattern of fashionable trends, collegiate fashions for men varied little from year to year during the decade. Prevailing definitions of masculinity insisted on a monolithic uniformity; war-related shortages certainly contributed to this stasis. Yet this uniformity, which touched even the smallest detail of the masculine wardrobe, only reinforced the pressure to "look the part." A Jockey advertisement urged men to take Jockey underwear to school to avoid looking too conspicuous in the locker room or dormitory. "At most good colleges and preps, Jockey is like a pair of slacks or an odd jacket—something that practically everybody wears."

Throughout the forties, the recommended outfit consisted of a wool plaid or striped Shetland jacket, gray flannel trousers, a pullover sweater, a foulard tie, and a button-down oxford shirt. The university style dictated that the jackets should be long (approximately 31½ inches) and pants short (ankle length). By the end of the decade, corduroy jackets made campus fashion news along with tweed caps. Cotton raincoats with raglan sleeves worn knee-length or just above the knee set the standard in outerwear. For colder climates, college men wrapped up in fleece-lined topcoats and tweed polo coats. Snap-brim hats and wool mufflers finished the look.

Undergraduates combined these classic articles of clothing with a few youthful fads. Students liked moccasin-style shoes with fringed flaps, penny loafers, and all-white oxfords. But for many students, saddle shoes were *the* choice. Men, like women, felt that the only saddle shoe worth wearing was the one that looked sufficiently worn. A writer for the *Daily Maroon* insisted that this issue was not open for discussion. If your saddle shoes were clean, you should "kick them around in the backyard a while until that greenhorn look has gone away."[61]

College men also shared their female classmates' desire for sweaters—lots of them. More comfortable and less formal than jackets, sweaters remained an indispensable part of the collegiate look. Men wore Shetland crewnecks, cardigans, and sleeveless pullovers. And the letter sweater remained a highly visible symbol of athletic prowess. Since sweaters were a staple item, undergraduates often selected neutral colors; but sweaters also gave men an opportunity to display some plumage. Brightly colored and richly patterned sweaters enlivened their wardrobes.

Above, in the privacy of the dorm, men, like women, dressed for comfort, not style. Right, at an informal event, such as this Syracuse University outing in 1948, men might substitute a colorful sweater or vest for suit and tie.

Although most college fashions could be described as understated, men broke with this rule in their choice of socks. If the colors of men's sweaters were loud, then their socks were thunderous. They were a popular gift, and girlfriends spent hours knitting intricately patterned argyles for their beaus. While describing the undergraduates' preference for short trousers in 1940, Henry Jackson, the fashion adviser for *Collier's*, explained that it was not to save material but rather "to show off their socks."[62] Seven years later, Jackson reported on the same trend more exuberantly. "When the lads want to burn the joint up they stick to Argyle socks in colors that would knock your eye out. . . . Wowsie!"[63]

Students followed established rules of sartorial etiquette on formal occasions. A 1940 article in *Collier's* summed up the benefits: "These three-piece outfits and accessories are calculated to blitzkrieg any dame. Anyway, short of a uniform, there's nothing gets the gals like the proper clothes for the proper occasion."[64] For "dates, dances, and occasionally visiting the dean," *Esquire* recommended a three-button suit in either gray flannel or a worsted glen plaid. Dinner dances and proms required a double- or single-breasted dinner jacket (preferably in midnight blue), cummerbund, black patent-leather shoes, suspenders, and white muffler. Warning its readers that "all too often roommates are either too tall or too short," the magazine's fashion editors encouraged men to arrive on campus with their own formal wardrobe.[65]

With the passage of the GI Bill, thousands of veterans, subsidized by the government, enrolled in college. Unlike younger students who concentrated on the social aspects of campus life, often at the expense of their studies, veterans were highly motivated to achieve academic excellence. They succeeded: veterans consistently made better grades than civilians.[66] Their impatience with college pranks and their reluctance to join in extracurricular activities also set veterans apart. In both their editorials and fashion commentary, men's magazines acknowledged the change. In a 1948 editorial, *Esquire* noted that the boys who thought it amusing to "drop two-hundred-pound cakes of ice down the stair well from the top floor now look pretty sad to the students who were loosing blockbusters over Berlin not very long ago."[67] The new undergraduates were older, often married with children, and "boldly striding into life instead of holing up for four years to escape from it."[68] A writer for *Collier's*, however, suggested that veterans might welcome the chance to enjoy the playfulness of college youth. "The uniform of our national Army was a noble garment. But it did little for the spirit. Any young man who has shuffled around in o.d.'s can be excused for wanting a sport coat that would shame the cockatoo."[69]

Collegiate styles provided a break from the conservative tone of men's clothing. Men allowed themselves the same scuffed saddle shoes women wore, with short pants to show off argyle socks, as shown by this 1947 University of North Carolina student (opposite).

For dates, men dressed up in two-piece suits or jackets and pressed trousers, as worn by these students at a Northwestern residence hall dance (below).

In 1946, a Seven Seas Triple-Duty Slacks advertisement appearing in *Esquire* targeted the concerns of GI Joes who wanted to look like Joe College. In the same issue, *Esquire* offered the veteran-scholar some advice on collegiate fashion so that he could look "less like an alumnus and more like an undergraduate." The basic wardrobe items were spelled out in great detail, including the recommendation of a tan jacket if "the wearing of khaki hasn't prejudiced him against it."[70]

Students of the 1940s differed markedly from their predecessors. Troubled by upheaval, undergraduates worried about their uncertain futures. The war shattered the insularity of college life; college could no longer serve as a carefree intermission between childhood and adulthood. World events also pushed ongoing struggles between students and administrators into the background. Unlike the collegians of the 1920s who celebrated their blatant disregard of tradition, students of the forties embraced conventionality. A distinctly youthful look asserted itself in men's preference for colorful socks, plaid flannel shirts, and multipatterned outfits, just as it did in the studied casualness of women's scuffed saddle shoes, rolled-up dungarees, and oversized sweaters. Yet, these were modest expressions of a campus spirit. As students scrambled for security in an insecure world, they chose conformity over conflict.

Students of the 1940s were eager to choose partners—for Saturday night and for life. Left, Northwestern students enjoy an informal dance. Above, Northwestern students Jo Baskin and Newton Minow celebrate getting pinned.

NOTES

1. Barbara M. Solomon, *In the Company of Educated Women* (New Haven: Yale University Press, 1985), 169.
2. Charlotte Huber, "Campus Into Camp," *Mademoiselle*, August 1941, 243.
3. Ellen K. Rothman, *Hearts and Hands: A History of Courtship in America* (Cambridge, MA: Harvard University Press, 1987), 299.
4. Huber, "Campus Into Camp," 242; "Mlle's Ten-Yearbook," *Mademoiselle*, February 1945, 165.
5. "Girl's ROTC," *Life*, January 11, 1943, 49.
6. W. W. Boyd, "The Unique Services of the Women's Colleges in Wartime," *School and Society*, September 1944, 474.
7. Ruth Sulzberger, "That Crumbling Ivory Tower," *New York Times Magazine*, March 14, 1943, 12.
8. Thomas N. Bonner, "The Unintended Revolution," *Change*, September/October 1986, 46.
9. Bonner, "The Unintended Revolution," 46.
10. Ruth Borneman, "Sororities: A Word for the Greeks," *Mademoiselle*, August 1939, 160.
11. Margaret Petsch, "Sororities: The Greek Tragedy," *Mademoiselle*, August 1939, 168.
12. "College Sororities," *Life*, December 17, 1945, 97.
13. Borneman, "Sororities," 164.
14. Petsch, "Sororities," 174.
15. "War's Effect on Campus," *Science News Letter*, March 1, 1947, 143.
16. "Lo, the Poor Co-Ed," *Newsweek*, April 29, 1942, 86.
17. Beth L. Bailey, *From Front Porch to Back Seat: Courtship in Twentieth-Century America* (Baltimore: Johns Hopkins Press, 1988), 36–37.
18. Judith Chase Churchill, "Your Chances of Getting Married," *Good Housekeeping*, October 1946, 38–39.
19. Henry Bowman, "Are Girls Becoming Pursuers?" *American Magazine*, April 1943, 102.
20. Dawn Crowell, "Passport to Popularity," *Ladies Home Journal*, September 1948, 249.
21. Marjorie Greenbaum, "That Non-Golden S-I-L-E-N-C-E!" *Seventeen*, March 1946, 142.
22. Mirra Komarovsky, "Cultural Contradictions and Sex Roles," *American Journal of Sociology*, November 1946, 185–87.
23. Helen Lefkowitz Horowitz, *Campus Life: Undergraduate Cultures from the End of the Eighteenth Century to the Present* (Chicago: University of Chicago Press, 1987), 216.
24. Solomon, *In the Company of Educated Women*, 194.
25. "Campus Correspondence," *Mademoiselle*, March 1949, 14.
26. "Chez E Phi," January 21, 1961, in *A E Phi Scrapbook*, 1949–50, Northwestern University Archives.
27. "Life Goes to the Pansy Breakfast," *Life*, July 23, 1945, 91.
28. Author interview with Josephine Baskin Minow, Northwestern University, Class of 1947, April 25, 1991.
29. Alice Beaton, "The Pond Grows Bigger," *Seventeen*, May 1946, 53.
30. Patricia Blake, "Why College Girls Dress that Way," *New York Times Magazine*, April 7, 1948, 23.
31. Anna E. Shively and Elizabeth D. Roseberry, "Adequacy of College Wardrobes Judged," *Journal of Home Economics*, February 1948, 81.
32. "She's the Type," *Mademoiselle*, August 1947, 239–41.
33. Author interview with Josephine Baskin Minow, April 25, 1991.
34. "Bobby-Sock Forum," *Newsweek*, October 30, 1944, 89.
35. Ellen Melinkoff, *What We Wore: An Offbeat Social History of Women's Clothing, 1950 to 1980* (New York: Quill, 1984), 197–98.
36. Anonymous, Vassar College, Class of 1948. Interview with author, March 22, 1991.
37. "If Your Daughter Had Her Way," *Good Housekeeping*, August 1941, 155–57.
38. Beaton, "The Pond Grows Bigger," 53.
39. Author interview with Suzanne Carter Meldman, Radcliffe College, Class of 1948, January 18, 1991.
40. "What's in a College Shop?" *Mademoiselle*, February 1940, 83.
41. "Gilding," *Purple Parrot*, December 1942, 27.
42. "The Lowdown on Collegiate . . . Fashions," *Pulse*, April 1947, 24.
43. "Instead of Saddle Shoes," *Good Housekeeping*, August 1941, 58.
44. Sidney McGiffert, "Vassar Vogues," *Mademoiselle*, May 1935, 13.
45. William A. H. Birnie, "The Truth about Co-eds," *American Magazine*, September 1940, 130.
46. Melva Lind, "So Your Daughter Is Away at College," *Hygeia*, January 1947, 69.
47. "Mlle's Freshman Chart," *Mademoiselle*, August 1941, 220–21.
48. Estelle Safier McBride, "Why College Girls Dress That Way," *New York Times Magazine*, December 10, 1944, 28.
49. *Willard Hall* (Evanston, IL: Northwestern University, 1948), Northwestern University Archives.
50. "News Item," *Daily Maroon*, April 6, 1945.
51. "Letter to the Editor," *Daily Maroon*, April 13, 1945.
52. McBride, "Why College Girls Dress That Way," 28.
53. "College Girls in Men's Clothing: Masculine Togs Invade Campus," *Life*, September 30, 1940, 41.
54. Jane Cobb, "Girls Will Be Boys," *New York Times Magazine*, November 3, 1940, 10.
55. *Daily Northwestern*, September 27, 1940, 12.
56. Blake, "Why College Girls Dress That Way," 23.
57. "Your Evening Dress—And How to Wear It!" *Seventeen*, November 1946, 136.
58. "Somebody's Looking at You—at College," *Mademoiselle*, August 1939.
59. Loren Flint, "Faddy Clothes Tabooed for Campus Wear," *Daily Maroon*, September 11, 1940.
60. "Bold but Neat is the Design for the Campus Wardrobe," *Esquire*, September 1948, 79, 82.
61. Flint, "Faddy Clothes Tabooed for Campus Wear."
62. Henry L. Jackson, "Back to School," *Collier's*, August 24, 1940, 13.
63. Henry L. Jackson, "Fall Guise," *Collier's*, August 23, 1947, 42.
64. Henry L. Jackson, "When It's a Date," *Collier's*, July 6, 1940.
65. "Campus Wearwithal," *Esquire*, September 1947, 105.
66. Horowitz, *Campus Life*, 185.
67. "Editorial: Turn Right at the Quonset Hut," *Esquire*, September 1948, 6.
68. Horowitz, *Campus Life*, 105; see also "Editorial: Old Man Axelrod Goes Back to School," *Esquire*, September 1947, 6.
69. Jackson, "Fall Guise," 42.
70. O. E. Schoeffler, "From Khaki to Campus," *Esquire*, September 1946, 113.

Heading off on a "tallyho," these students dressed for the occasion. The decorative embellishments, fragile fabrics, and oversized hats of most of the women provide a striking contrast to the tailored skirts and mannish boaters worn by the other coeds. The men wear straw hats to break up the formality of their dress suits.

College regulations required that students dress up for dinner, and this rose gauze two-piece dress would have been a fashionable choice in the 1890s. Although the walking suit (inset) follows the same silhouette with its exaggeraed leg-of-mutton sleeves and bell-shaped skirt, its shortened hemline, durable fabric, and mix-and-match potential made it a more practical choice for students' daytime routine.

This wool challis dressing gown and matching crocheted slippers (inset) were part of Chicagoan Jessie Clara Ward's 1890s college wardrobe. Worn in the dormitory for late-night entertaining or studying, the loose-fitting wrapper would have been a welcome change from constricting corsets and layered petticoats.

Fitting in during the 1920s meant keeping pace with an ever-changing parade of campus fads. While the raccoon coat remained a popular fashion both on and off campus throughout the decade, unbuckled galoshes were distinctly collegiate. Plus fours, knickers that fell four inches below the knee, were also popular on college campuses. Some colleges, such as Princeton, developed their own rules about who could wear plus fours as a way to distinguish upperclassmen from freshmen.

The dropped waist and body-skimming silhouette of this ivory silk dress accented the slender body type of the ideal 1920s flapper. To coeds, the new fashions were sensual, modern, and liberating. A felt cloche pulled low over a sleek bobbed hairstyle completed the ensemble. Molded pleats and handpainted flowers (inset) provided variation in the hat's design. Collegiate men were also trendsetters; this man's raw silk suit and straw boater hat reinforced the youthful look of the 1920s.

For students of the 1940s, date night meant dressing according to the rigid fashion rules of the decade. Women donned tailored dresses and pearls, while men made an impression in dark suits and patterned ties. In this decade, teenage styles emerged as a distinct fashion category. For relaxing with friends, women enjoyed the comfort of oversized sweatshirts, rolled-up dungarees, and saddle shoes (inset).

During the 1940s, the most coveted winter coats were made of fur. Any coed wearing this Persian-lamb coat with matching muff and hat would have been at the height of fashion. Men and women built their college wardrobes around sweaters (inset). The letter on his sweater, symbolizing athletic accomplishment, continued the tradition begun in the late nineteenth century.

Youthful fashions such as the thigh-high hemline of this suede miniskirt shocked the older generation in the 1960s; fishnet stockings drew even more attention to women's legs (inset). Women could also opt for the slightly longer hemline of the plaid skirt. Not all students dressed as campus radicals, and men's suits, now cut closer to the body, still had a place in many students' closets.

Students in the 1960s used clothing to make a political statement. Patched denim, long hair, and ethnic jewelry set youths apart from the Establishment. The peace sign became the symbol of a generation as students protested U.S. involvement in the Vietnam War. Originally worn as a sign of solidarity among political youths, the peace symbol lost its meaning as manufacturers used it to emblazon everything from sandals to rugs (inset).

60

Youths at Woodstock tuned in and turned on. With their Indian-print fabrics, unisex T-shirts, and beat-up jeans, they made a deliberate antifashion statement.

The Times They Are A-Changin':
College Life in the 1960s

Bob Dylan's words became the theme of a generation. Change was everywhere in the sixties. College and university administrators were forced to watch as students challenged the governance and the meaning of higher education. Parents found themselves on the wrong side of the generation gap as they witnessed the transformation of their children into hedonistic, androgynous strangers. And students asserted their independence by building a vocabulary around sex, drugs, and rock and roll.

When undergraduates in the 1960s defended campus activities, chances are they were not referring to the debate team, sororities, or the banjo club. Students for a Democratic Society meetings, antiwar demonstrations, and civil rights marches aroused this generation of students. With a growing sense of alienation and a rising commitment to activism, students demanded to be heard. Dissent led to protest; protest led to revolt.

Within a few short years, tensions escalated to a point where officials could no longer control campus events. The protests that resulted in violence received the most publicity. Campus authorities at schools such as Columbia, Berkeley, and the University of Wisconsin called in police and the National Guard to stop the strikes and the sit-ins.

Change was the hallmark of the sixties. In 1965, DePaul students still wore the traditional freshman beanies (right). By the late sixties, University of Illinois students taunted National Guardsmen with impunity (opposite). In 1970, graduating Smith students decorated their gowns with doves of peace (below).

In this period of upheaval, students denounced long-standing college traditions as anachronistic and irrelevant. In 1969, a woman at DePaul University in Chicago challenged the notion of the freshman beanie in the college's underground newspaper. "Imagine, the boys among us might be fighting and dying in a war if they weren't here. And you expect them to carry on tradition (?) by wearing some idiotic beanie?"[1] Graduating classes in 1970 protested the nation's involvement in the Vietnam War by appearing at commencement in gowns and mortarboards decorated with peace symbols. By the end of the sixties, everyone seemed to be pointing fingers at college youth and asking, "Who are they?"

Undergraduates of the 1960s were the products of the baby boom. Insulated by the affluence of postwar prosperity and doted on by parents trained by Dr. Spock, this army of youth came of age during the sixties. Committed to providing a better life for their children, parents embraced the promise of a college degree. Between 1963 and 1973, enrollment in all institutions of higher learning more than doubled. By 1973, there were 9.6 million college students in this country.[2] For the first time in American history, going to college was a common expectation, "one more often unquestionably obeyed than defied."[3]

Of this mammoth group of collegians, 5 to 10 percent of the student population qualified as activists. Even at its height of popularity, Students for a Democratic Society estimated a dues-paying membership of only fifty-five hundred.[4] As children of the affluent middle class, the most radical undergraduates enjoyed the luxury of financial security and the benefits of education. In the words of the University of Michigan newspaper, activists "took their tactics from Gandhi, their idealism from philosophy class and their money from Daddy."[5]

Most students, however, rejected the principles of political and cultural extremism. When *Life* magazine visited Indiana University in 1967 in search of revolutionaries, they found instead students who played it safe and enjoyed fanciful characters such as Snoopy and Tolkien's hobbits.[6] Yet radical leaders could mobilize their peers into action for the right cause. In 1969, students held strikes in at least 350 colleges and universities with the intent of disrupting or halting classes, and over half the campuses nationwide experienced some kind of student demonstration.[7]

The uprising in Berkeley during the freedom summer of 1964 marked the beginning of student revolt, but the roots of student activism can be found in the civil rights movement of the late fifties and early sixties. Disaffected students, black and white, supported the political goals of the movement. The social struggles of African-Americans gave form to the students' own feelings of powerlessness and alienation. That

several incidents involved college students cemented their feelings of community. In 1960, a waitress at a Woolworth lunch counter in Greensboro, North Carolina, told four black students from North Carolina Agricultural and Technical College, "We don't serve colored here." The students refused to leave. As students joined in, the fight against racial discrimination grew to be hundreds, and then thousands, strong. Students organized voter registration drives in the South during summer vacations, raised funds, and protested segregationist actions and discrimination on campuses all across the country.[8]

Students discovered the power of their collective voice in the process. Adopting the rhetoric and strategies of the civil rights movement, students prepared their assault on the university system. These youths were committed to political action through confrontation, and peaceful demonstrations sometimes yielded to violent clashes with authority. Angered by a burgeoning list of societal offenses and feverish for change, students attacked the Establishment. They protested the corporate state, racial discrimination, and the destruction of the environment. Materialism, hypocrisy, and apathy were, they claimed, the results of a soulless culture, the products of a system that reduced individuals to a computer card that came with the warning, "Do not fold, spindle, or mutilate." And for this system the students indicted the older generation.

Protests occurred on campuses large and small. Left and right, activists at Northwestern University. Opposite, in 1969 political activists encouraged North Park College students to join the many campuses protesting the United States' involvement in the Vietnam War.

For a brief time in 1968, college campuses belonged to student dissidents. At Tuskegee Institute, students held twelve trustees captive for several hours.[9] The same year, 120 black students at Northwestern seized the university's finance office and maintained control for over thirty-eight hours.[10] On many campuses, members of Students for a Democratic Society organized freshman "disorientation tours." The highlights at Columbia included a view of the newly installed bulletproof windows in the president's office and instructions on how to break into an administration building.[11] Some university presidents had no choice but to stop classes and cancel final exams. School administrators soon countered with carefully worded policies of student rights and regulations; summaries of civil law and detailed procedures of disciplinary committees appeared in freshman orientation packets. In the first wave of assaults, however, administrators bowed under the weight of student demands.

For legions of undergraduates, the Vietnam War was the catalyst that incited them to action. The war turned bureaucratic ills into societal crimes, and revolt became an appropriate response. Incensed by the televised brutality of the war, students denounced the war as immoral. And because of increased draft calls and a Selective Service system that offered only temporary deferments, young men had to confront the possibility that they, too, would be part of the war. Anxiety over their futures turned apolitical students into campus activists. Collectively and often with the support of faculty, students defied, dodged, and disrupted the Selective Service system.[12]

In their battles against perceived injustices on campus, students fought to seize control of their personal lives. One of the first issues they addressed was parietal hours. Since their beginnings, institutions of higher education had accepted the responsibilities of parental surrogates. Historically, as part of their effort to regulate interaction between the sexes, college and university officials established curfews, enforced sign-out policies, and policed on-campus activities.

When students arrived on campus in the sixties, they encountered long-standing policies designed to restrict the amount of time men and women spent together and to discourage sexual activity. During visiting hours, for example, doors had to be kept open the width of a wastebasket, and couples had to have their feet on the floor at all times. Collegians of the 1940s and 1950s certainly tested these boundaries, but their rebellion lacked the force of a generationwide attack. In the early 1950s, approximately four of five women had remained virgins throughout their college years; by the 1970s, only one of five graduating women had.[13]

Students discovered the power of collective action during the civil rights protests of the late 1950s and early 1960s. Black students remained active in the black power and antiwar movements. Above, banner at North Park College. Right, students at Northwestern.

With the sexual revolution of the 1960s, permissiveness was in the air and the Pill was readily available. Students demanded their rights as adults whose moral codes should be self-determined and self-regulated.

A significant shift in attitudes occurred in the sixties, and college youth were among the first to express it.[14] Students of the 1960s separated physical intimacy from the pinning-engagement-marriage trilogy and dismissed monogamy as an "uptight" notion. Coeds challenged their role as sexual referees, men questioned the appeal of "nice girls," and both sexes espoused a philosophy of guilt-free sex. "We've discarded the idea that the loss of virginity is related to degeneracy," said an Ohio State senior.[15]

Against a background of students singing, "Let's spend the night together," college administrators struggled to defend the relevance of their rules. A student at the University of Illinois mocked the school's "three foot rule," which required a couple to keep three of their collective four feet on the floor at all times. It "does not make for better morals," he said, "only more convoluted romantic gymnastics." A resourceful sophomore at Oberlin College circumvented the school's wastebasket policy by selling precrushed cans "guaranteed to keep your door open less than 3 inches." And Harvard's policy of restricting women's weekday visits to three hours in the afternoons prompted one senior to note: "I know people around here who think the rhythm method means every afternoon from 4 to 7."[16]

Enforcement became more of a problem as student resistance grew increasingly defiant. At the University of Chicago in 1966, the student government spoke out against the indignity of women's parietal hours.

Coed dorm, Oberlin College, 1970. Once the initial thrill subsided, many students confessed that coed living actually deemphasized sex.

Castigating the administration for its Victorian double standard, the student government president called for women to break the rules. "If everyone suddenly stopped obeying them, they would cease to exist."[17]

Up against the wall, administrators began to ease their policies. University of Colorado students cried "free at last" when the school abolished parietal rules in 1969. Yet the elimination of visiting hours was just the beginning. In the flush of their sexual awakening, students on many campuses demanded a more drastic change: coeducational dormitories. Oberlin College was one of the first to adopt such a program of "calculated permissiveness."[18] Other schools soon fell in line. Praising the social advantages of coeducational living, administrators tried to allay parental fears of sexual promiscuity.

Once the initial thrill subsided, many students confessed that coed living actually deemphasized sex. The daily routine turned "forbidden fruit" into friends. As one Stanford junior asked, "When was the last time you heard of a panty raid in a coed dorm?"[19] In 1971, three women described their campus experience for *Seventeen* magazine. Praising coed dormitories, a student from Hampshire College in Massachusetts declared, "I no longer size up every boy I meet as a potential husband. . . . I am not obsessed with boys or getting dates."[20] Familiarity was not an instant aphrodisiac. When a writer for *Look* magazine visited the first coed fraternity at Stanford in 1969, she found not orgies but a group of men reevaluating their attitudes toward women. "It used to be that you'd see a girl looking awful and think, 'Ugh, I don't want to go out with her.' Now, if you see a girl from the house looking bad, you go over and put your arm around her shoulder and ask her what's the matter."[21]

Students' complaints about dorm life went beyond issues of morality. The very notion of living by someone else's rules rankled. How could this group of young people, who perceived centralized authority as a societal straitjacket, resolve living within four cinder-block walls and the rules that went with them? For a growing number of students, the only solution was to move out of the dormitory. University of Chicago students summarized the advantages of off-campus housing in their 1968 yearbook as "the freedom, maybe to smoke pot or invite your girl over for the night. The freedom to go to hell in your handbasket. The will may not be there, but the option is."[22]

Administrators wrestled with the limits of their authority. Should they (and could they) continue to act in loco parentis? Theory was put to the test in 1968 when Linda Leclair, a sophomore at Barnard College, announced that she was living off campus with her boyfriend, a Columbia junior. Barnard expelled the student immediately. Unrepentant, Leclair stood firm. After months of national press coverage, Barnard issued a compromise. On the recommendation of a student-faculty committee, Leclair was allowed to return to school with the stipulation that she be barred from the snack bar, the cafeteria, and the recreation room.[23]

Not only were students exploring their bodies—they were expanding their minds. Their quest for self-discovery often turned psychedelic as marijuana and LSD replaced alcohol as the drugs of choice.[24] According to one student, "You might as well face it. If you're going to college, you'll probably smoke pot."[25]

Students lauded the personal and social benefits of turning on. Parents listened with shock, fear, and disbelief, which only increased students' pleasure. In a rambling article that appeared in the DePaul underground newspaper, a student tried to describe the "substantial rewards" of getting stoned. "Drugs are an important part of my life. . . . Records seem easier to understand and for a change the lyrics make sense."[26] Another student at the University of Missouri shared his LSD-related insights with *Look* magazine. "[Before] I wanted to make a lot of money and have a comfortable life. Now . . . I want happiness and peace. . . . I have a lot more fun looking at flowers now than before. I've really gotten caught up with the sky and sunsets."[27]

Smoking grass was part of a student's rite of passage, a password into the counterculture's inner circle. One woman described the pressures she felt to conform in her early years at Yale: "Drugs have become . . . a symbol for who you are, and you can't be . . . Progressive and Creative and Free Thinking without taking that crumpled role of dry brown vegetation and holding it to your lips." Her refusal to participate in the drug culture made her suspect. "Often I'm spoken to almost as a foreigner . . . as if I were a teacher or a parent or a college admissions officer."[28]

As students deviated from established values, the gray areas of indecision disappeared. A student was either in or out, right or left, hip or square. Emblems of alienation and allegiance vibrated with political overtones. For all students, clothing served as communication. Most undergraduates agreed on one guiding principle: the old sartorial rules had to be shattered. The counterculture reviled the manicured styles of the fifties and early sixties as unnatural. From their perspective, teased and lacquered hair, heavily armored foundation garments, and three-inch heels embodied the repressive attitudes of the Establishment. The image of a sea of suburban men waiting for the train in their look-alike suits, hats, and briefcases was equally repugnant.

Below left, residents of an off-campus house at Northwestern in 1971 display popular counter-culture fashions—long skirts or jeans for women, jeans for men, and long hair for everyone. Below right, accessories for such costumes might include love beads, a macrame belt, or a headband.

As they dressed up in fantasy garb or dressed down in work clothes, students playfully experimented with various identities. Clothing became costume, turning student "happenings" into theatrical events. At one 1967 Berkeley party, students wore "Edwardian velvet gowns, spaceman suits, African robes, cowboy regalia, Donald Duck hats and Indian war paint."[29] Students countered and toppled the tyranny of fashion with outrageous and inexpensive antifashion statements. Students played dress-up, except this time it was a fantasy wardrobe, not Mommy's closet, that they raided.

Jeans symbolized the counterculture's rejection of materialism, and students built their wardrobes around them. During the 1940s and 1950s, students claimed jeans, or dungarees as they called them, as a style of the youth culture, but no one was prepared for the denim explosion of the sixties. Students who wanted to express solidarity with the working class "dressed righteous and 'with the people.'"[30] Others wore jeans because everyone else did.

Men and women zipped themselves into tight jeans that softened with age and conformed to the body. Students took these mass-produced goods and individualized them with embroidered and painted designs or colorful patches. As the quintessential expression of the new consciousness and stripped of distinctions of status, jeans broke down barriers of difference and affirmed the "new unity of youth."[31] Demanding the right to do their own thing, students discovered, however, that most of their peers wanted to do the *same* thing.

The sartorial language of individuality became another symbol of conformity. Inevitably, students overestimated the power of dress. A change in consciousness required more than a change of clothing, which became all too evident by the mid-1970s, when manufacturers affixed designer labels to the backsides of jeans. On the strength of a mass-produced signature, the clothing of the people became another status commodity.

Below left, Northwestern students, c. 1975, share a joint in a room decorated with tie-dyed hangings and Indian-print bedspreads. Below right, a senior at Scripps College appropriates the flag as fashion. Right, through their mockery, students turned symbols of patriotism into emblems of pacifism.

From the adult perspective, students' clothing choices turned the world upside down. Where did patched blue jeans and bare feet fit into the neatly pressed, buttoned-down world of the organization man? And how could a coiffed, shirtwaisted mother relate to her newly blossomed flower child in peasant dresses and love beads? Even if parents wanted to meet their children eye to eye, the long curtains of hair made that impossible.

The anger that forced the two generations into different camps crystallized over the issue of men's hairstyles. Since the early nineteenth century, men had worn their hair shorter than women. Hair length was an absolute gender symbol. But in the mid-sixties, youthful radicals began to challenge this convention. At first, men grew their hair long in front and shaggy around the ears after the trend set by British rock groups. Soon, hair fell to the chin and, in some cases, even to the shoulders.

As more men trespassed the established gender boundaries, the debate grew increasingly hostile. One rebel expressed his delight with the controversy. "I want everyone to see me and say 'There goes an enemy of the state,' because that's where I'm at, as we say in the Revolution biz."[32] When parents hurled the familiar epithet, "You look like a girl" at their long-haired son, they questioned his masculinity as well as his politics. Young men, in turn, reveled in the uproar.

Long hair symbolized pacifism and a rejection of tradition. And the girls loved it.

Hair also became a symbol of racial identity and ethnic consciousness. The evolution of the civil rights movement into the black power movement triggered an awareness of black heritage among African-Americans, an awareness that was celebrated in dress and fashion. Tired of playing the beauty game by white people's rules, African-Americans celebrated their racial characteristics and grew Afros, or "naturals." Repudiating hair straighteners and bleaching creams, they proudly asserted that black is beautiful.[33]

When Barnard women chanted "Up Against the Wall Mother————" to police during the Columbia uprising, they left little doubt that ideas of femininity were also changing.[34] By the end of the decade, the emerging women's liberation movement had gained momentum on college campuses. In defiance of gender conventions, female activists rejected the trappings of artifice, adopting a decidedly "unfeminine" look. In their dress, University of Chicago coeds embraced the notion that the personal is the political. Not everyone approved. According to the 1962 *Cap & Gown*, University of Chicago women wore clothes "as if they were homework assignments, assignments they have flunked. . . . Style, to a UC woman, carries only its literary sense."[35]

Police remove a protester at Northwestern in 1969 (below left), and in 1971 a restaurant displays its "No hippies allowed" policy on the front door (below right). Opposite, by 1974 denim was moving from political statement to fashion statement.

Dress did more than distinguish generations; it drew irreconcilable boundaries around opposing on-campus philosophies. "If you were aware and hip, you wore bell bottoms. If you were a nerd, you didn't."[36] Counterculture symbols grew so pervasive that getting dressed in the morning became a political act. People were judged by their wardrobes, not their words. "You couldn't get into a women's liberation meeting in a skirt (let alone a tie) or into a student radical meeting with a crew cut or into a black power session with processed hair."[37]

Women in the sixties could choose from a variety of looks. There was the proletarian costume of low-slung jeans, T-shirts, and work boots, which *Glamour* described with the hyperactive adjectives of fashion reportage: "Do wear the Army-Navy store look, sporty jean jackets and snug white T's, straight-legged pants slung from wide garrison belts, husky workmen's boots. Wonderful with it, a man-size watch."[38] A woman could also opt for the teasing sexuality of thigh-high skirts and skinny, ribbed pullovers. If a student wanted to get back to nature, she could wear a granny gown or an Indian block-print skirt with sandals and handcrafted jewelry.[39] In all guises, women's clothing moved with the body. Fringed vests, tie-dyed scarves, floppy hats, and multiple strands of love beads defied the restrained fashions of the older generation.

Browse through a 1969 college yearbook and compare the photographs of activists with those of the Young Republicans. While the former raided army-navy surplus stores and secondhand "boutiques," the latter continued to purchase back-to-school wardrobes. They color-coordinated their miniskirts and A-line dresses with fishnet stockings and "chunky" shoes. And fraternity and sorority pins still found a place on monogrammed blouses and sweaters. Villager round-collared blouses with matching heather wool sweaters, Bass moccasins, Pappagallo flats—these were magical names for the conservatively dressed coed. Her male counterpart dressed in chino pants, oxford shirts, and wool blazers.

Inevitably, student garb became a uniform with the strings of conformity firmly attached. The icons of revolution lost their meaning when the mainstream wore them to fit in instead of to stand out and make a statement. Students who started out "democratized by denim" in the 1960s ended up homogenized in designer jeans by the mid-1970s. The artifacts of the sixties, however, continue to attract and enthrall some.[40] Recycled and reinterpreted, they still carry the mythology of the era:

> Just the other day I came out of a health-food store in Venice. A young couple came toward me. His hair was long and unruly, and he wore a jeans jacket, a pink shirt, and a scarf for a headband. She had let her punk haircut grow out, and she was wearing a long skirt of several fabrics, an Indian gauze blouse, a flowing shawl, several necklaces, bracelets, and other bangles. They made me so happy. I went running home shouting, "I told you, I told you . . . the sixties are coming back!"[41]

Not everyone embraced the dress of the radical youths. Northwestern's 1969 Syllabus *displays neatly dressed Nixon supporters (below left); many students continued to dress in updated versions of the sweaters and skirts and the suits and ties of the forties and fifties (below right). Opposite, Northwestern student, 1971. Many students took mass-produced jeans and individualized them by embroidering them or making cut-off shorts.*

NOTES

1. Catherine Wenninger, "If you think you can exploit freshmen . . . ," *Aletheia*, October 15, 1969, 4.
2. Landon Y. Jones, *Great Expectations: America & the Baby Boom Generation* (New York: Coward, McCann & Geoghagen, 1980), 82.
3. Esther Raushenbush, "From Where I Sit," *Mademoiselle*, January 1968, 130.
4. "The Graduate: Snapshots of Three Generations," *Newsweek*, June 24, 1968, 70.
5. "Why Those Students Are Protesting," *Time*, May 3, 1968, 25.
6. Gerald Moore, "Who Says College Kids Have Changed?" *Life*, May 19, 1967, 95.

7. Helen Lefkowitz Horowitz, *Campus Life: Undergraduate Cultures from the End of the Eighteenth Century to the Present* (Chicago:University of Chicago Press, 1987), 221.
8. Peter G. Filene, *Him/Her/Self: Sex Roles in Modern America*, 2nd ed. (Baltimore: The Johns Hopkins University Press, 1986), 184.
9. "Anarchy Spreads in U.S. Colleges," *U.S. News and World Report*, May 6, 1968, 65.
10. Jack N. Porter, *Student Protest and the Technocratic Society: The Case of ROTC* (Chicago: Adams Press, 1973), 53.
11. "Campus Rebels: Who, Why, What," *Newsweek*, September 30, 1968, 63.
12. W. J. Rorabaugh, *Berkeley at War: The 1960s* (New York: Oxford University Press, 1989), 114–15.
13. Filene, *Him/Her/Self*, 203.
14. Ellen K. Rothman, *Hands and Hearts: A History of Courtship in America* (New York: Basic Books, 1987), 306–10.
15. "The Morals Revolution on the U.S. Campus," *Newsweek*, April 6, 1964, 52.
16. "The Necker Checkers," *Newsweek*, May 8, 1967, 96.
17. Joan Phillips, "SG Urges Open Revolt Against Women's Hours," *Daily Maroon*, September 30, 1966.
18. "An Intimate Revolution in Campus Life," *Life*, November 20, 1970, 32–38.
19. "Boys and Girls Together," *Time*, May 30, 1969, 44.
20. "Away From Home," *Seventeen*, August 1971, 102.
21. Betty Rollin, "New Hang-up For Parents: Co-Ed Living," *Look*, September 23, 1969, 27.
22. University of Chicago *Cap & Gown*, 1968, 23.
23. Charles Kaiser, *1968 in America: Music, Politics, Chaos, Counterculture, and the Shaping of a Generation* (New York: Weidenfeld Nicolson, 1988), 255.
24. Horowitz, *Campus Life*, 228.
25. Jack Shepherd, "Potheads in Missouri," *Look*, August 8, 1967, 15.
26. "Games on Grass, Insight on Acid," *Aletheia*, May 15, 1968, 2.
27. Shepherd, "Potheads in Missouri," 17.
28. Joyce Maynard, *Looking Back: A Chronicle of Growing Up Old in the Sixties* (New York: Avon Books, 1972), 133–34.
29. Sara Davidson, *Loose Change: Three Women of the Sixties* (New York: Pocket Books, 1978), 139.
30. Tom Wolfe, *Radical Chic & Mau-Mauing the Flak Catchers* (New York: Farrar, Strauss, and Giroux, 1970), 126.
31. Charles Reich, *The Greening of America* (New York: Random House, 1970), 234–39.
32. James Simon Kunen, *The Strawberry Statement* (New York: Avon Books, 1968), 86.
33. Valery Giddings, "Campus Dress of the 1960's," in Barbara M. Starke, Lillian O. Holloman, and Barbara K. Nordquist, *African American Dress and Adornment: A Cultural Perspective* (Iowa: Kendall/Hunt Publishing Company, 1990), 152–53.
34. "The Graduate," 71.
35. University of Chicago *Cap & Gown*, 1962, 140.
36. Ellen Melinkoff, *What We Wore: An Offbeat Social History of Women's Clothing, 1950 to 1980* (New York: Quill, 1984), 159.
37. Ellen Goodman, *Close to Home* (New York: Fawcett Crest, 1979), 38–39.
38. "Uni-sex," *Newsweek*, February 14, 1966, 59.
39. Rorabaugh, *Berkeley at War*, 133–34.
40. Richard Goldstein, *Reporting the Counterculture* (Boston: Unwin Hyman, 1989), xiv.
41. Melinkoff, *What We Wore*, 164.

Illustration Credits

viii, Smith College Archives; ix, Illustration House, Inc.; x, Ralph Crane, *Life* magazine, ©1945, Time Warner Inc.; xi, University of Chicago Special Collections; xii, CHS, ICHi-22541; 1 left, Wellesley College Archives; 1 center and right, CHS Costume Collection; 2 above, CHS Costume Collection; 2 below, Wellesley College Archives; 3 left, George Washington University Archives; 3 right, Smith College Archives; 4 left, Smith College Archives; 4 right, CHS Costume Collection; 5 above, Smith College Archives; 5 below, Wellesley College Archives; 6 above, Smith College Archives; 6 below, *Life at Vassar*, n.d., Vassar College Library, George B. Shattuck, photographer; 7, Wellesley College Archives; 8, CHS Costume Collection; 9 above, North Park College Archives; 9 below, Smith College Archives; 10, Northwestern University Archives; 11 left, *Legenda*, 1909, Wellesley College Archives; 11 right, *Syllabus*, 1892, Northwestern University Archives; 12, Smith College Archives; 13 left, Smith College Archives; 13 right, from Lossing, *History of Vassar College and Its Founder*, n.d., Vassar College Library; 14, Smith College Archives; 15 above and below, Wellesley College Archives; 16, top, middle, and bottom, Wellesley College Archives; 17, Smithsonian Institution Costume Division, #91-6775; 18, *Purple Parrot*, April 1927, Northwestern University Archives; 19 left, *Cherry Tree*, 1925, George Washington University Archives; 19 right, *Cherry Tree*, 1927, George Washington University Archives; 20 left, Northwestern University Archives; 20 right, *Purple Parrot*, March 1927, Northwestern University Archives; 21 left, *Purple Parrot*, January 1927, Northwestern University Archives; 21 right, *Illio*, 1929, University of Illinois Archives; 22, *DePaulian*, 1925, DePaul University Archives; 23, flask lent by Newton Minow; 24 left, *Purple Parrot*, April 1927, Northwestern University Archives; 24 right, *Syllabus*, 1926, Northwestern University Archives; 25 left, *Illio*, 1925, University of Illinois Archives; 25 right, *DePaulian*, 1925, DePaul University Archives; 26 above, Northwestern University Archives; 26 below, *Cherry Tree*, 1925, George Washington University Archives; 27, *Illio*, 1925, University of Illinois Archives; 28 left, Smithsonian Institution Costume Division, #78-10538; 28 right, *Illio*, 1928, University of Illinois Archives; 29 above, *DePaulian*, 1925, DePaul University Archives; 29 below, CHS, ICHi-14231; 30, *Syllabus*, 1929, Northwestern University Archives; 31, courtesy of Hartmarx; 32, *Yale Record*, October 23, 1923, Yale University Archives; 33, *Purple Parrot*, October 1926, Northwestern University Archives; 34, Northwestern University Archives, James Bixby, photographer; 35 above and below right, University of Chicago Special Collections; 35 below left, Mundelein College Archives; 36 above, courtesy of Library of Congress; 36 below, Alfred Eisenstaedt, *Life* magazine, ©1943, Time Warner Inc.; 37 left, *Chicago Tribune*, May 12, 1946, University of Chicago Special Collections; 37 right, *Syllabus*, 1946, Northwestern University Archives; 38, Northwestern University Archives; 39, Northwestern University Archives; 40 left, sorority and fraternity pins, top lent by Ruth Moss Buck, middle and bottom lent by Mrs. Sumner Sollitt; 40 center, *Cupola*, 1942, North Park College Archives; 40 right, Smithsonian Institution Costume Division, #75-1773; 41 left, CHS Costume Collection; 41 center, *Yackety Yack*, 1949, University of North Carolina–Chapel Hill; 41 right, Peter Stackpole, *Life* magazine, ©1945, Time Warner Inc.; 42, *Good Housekeeping*, August 1941; 43 left, Smith College Archives; 43 right, CHS, ICHi-22536; 44, University of Chicago Special Collections; 45 below left, University of Chicago Special Collections; 45 below right, *Yackety Yack*, 1947, University of North Carolina–Chapel Hill; 46 left, courtesy of Hartmarx; 46 right, Northwestern University Archives; 47 left, CHS, ICHi-22540; 47 right, Smithsonian Institution Costume Division, #79-5228; 48, *Yackety Yack*, 1947, University of North Carolina–Chapel Hill; 49, Northwestern University Archives; 50 left, Northwestern University Archives, James Bixby, photographer; 50 right, courtesy of Jo Minow; 52, CHS, ICHi-14231; 53, cotton-and-silk gauze two-piece dress, 1894, gift of Estelle F. Ward, CHS Costume Collection;

53, wool tweed walking suit, 1894, gift of Estelle F. Ward, CHS Costume Collection; 54, wool dressing gown, 1894, gift of Estelle F. Ward, CHS Costume Collection; 54, crocheted bedroom slippers, 1894, gift of Estelle F. Ward, CHS Costume Collection; 55, wool herringbone jacket, 1927, gift of Mrs. Arthur Hoffheimer, CHS Costume Collection; 55, tweed knickers, 1923, gift of Mrs. Bernard Iddings Bell, CHS Costume Collection; 55, wool motoring cap, c. 1925, gift of Mr. and Mrs. Philip K. Wrigley, CHS Costume Collection; 55, raccoon coat, c. 1925, gift of Mrs. Otto Madlener, CHS Costume Collection; 55, tweed skirt and tan silk blouse, c. 1927, gift of Kate Gregg, CHS Costume Collection; 55, black felt cloche, 1925, gift of Kate Gregg, CHS Costume Collection; 55, wool coat with fur collar, c. 1923, gift of Mrs. D. D. Hamacheck, CHS Costume Collection; 55, green wool cloche with band, 1925, gift of Kate Gregg, CHS Costume Collection; 55, leather boots with fur trim, c. 1925, gift of Edward B. Kelley, CHS Costume Collection; 56, raw silk suit, c. 1929, gift of Mrs. C. Phillip Miller, CHS Costume Collection; 56, straw boater hat, c. 1920, gift of Mrs. Howard Linn, CHS Costume Collection; 56, silk crepe dress with silk embroidery, c. 1925, gift of Mrs. Lawrence E. Norem, CHS Costume Collection; 56, blue straw cloche, c. 1924, gift of estate of Anna Emery Hanson, CHS Costume Collection; 56, rose wool cloche, c. 1929, gift of Mrs. Edwin Brand III, CHS Costume Collection; 56, ivory wool cloche with stenciled floral design, c. 1925, CHS Costume Collection; 57, wool double-breasted suit, 1943, gift of Mrs. Robert C. Peck, CHS Costume Collection; 57, wool dress, c. 1945, gift of Mrs. James M. Hopkins, CHS Costume Collection; 57, Northwestern cotton sweatshirt, c. 1945, gift of Ruth Moss Buck, CHS Costume Collection; 57, women's jeans, c. 1945, gift of Ruth Moss Buck, CHS Costume Collection; 58, Persian-lamb coat, hat, and muff, c. 1943, gift of estate of Margaret M. Kruty, CHS Costume Collection; 58, University of North Carolina letter seater, 1946–47, lent by F. William Spiegel, Jr.; 58, cashmere sweater, c. 1950, gift of Kate Gregg, CHS Costume Collection; 58, wool skirt, c. 1945, gift of Mrs. James M. Hopkins, CHS Costume Collection; 59, suede miniskirt, 1971, gift of Rena Benrubi-Abrams, CHS Costume Collection; 59, accessories, 1969, lent by Amy Waller Anderson; 59, wool suit, c. 1967, gift of Andrew Leo, CHS Costume Collection; 59, sweater with matching plaid skirt, c. 1970, gift of Mr. and Mrs. Eugene Kwas, CHS Costume Collection; 60, blue and yellow floral cotton shirt, c. 1970, lent by Sharon Smith; 60, suede vest with fringe, c. 1972, lent by Walter Reinhardt; 60, Indian-print cotton blouse, c. 1972, lent by Sharon Smith; 60, patched denim skirt, 1970, lent by Nancy Lerman; 60, peace sandals, c. 1968, gift of Mrs. Oscar Gerber, CHS Costume Collection; 60, peace tie, c. 1970, gift of Mr. Brooks McCormick, Jr., CHS Costume Collection; peace ring, c. 1967, gift of Jo Hopkins Deutsch, CHS Costume Collection; 60, peace rug, c. 1970, lent by Mary Rose Minow; 61, Bill Eppridge, *Life* magazine, ©Time Warner Inc.; 62, University of Illinois Archives; 63 above, *DePaulian*, 1965, DePaul University Archives; 63 below, Smith College Archives; 64 left, Northwestern University Archives; 64 right, *Syllabus*, 1969, Northwestern University Archives; 65, North Park College Archives; 66 above, North Park College Archives; 66 below, Northwestern University Archives; 67, Bill Ray, *Life* magazine, ©1970, Time Warner Inc.; 68 left, *Syllabus*, 1971, Northwestern University Archives; 68 right, CHS Costume Collection; 69 above, *DePaulian*, 1971, DePaul University Archives; 69 below left, Northwestern University Archives; 69 below right, Smithsonian Institution Costume Division, #89-4914; 70 left, *Syllabus*, 1969, Northwestern University Archives; 70 right, *Syllabus*, 1971, Northwestern University Archives; 71, *Syllabus*, 1974, Northwestern University Archives; 72 left, *Syllabus*, 1969, Northwestern University Archives; 72 right, Loyola University Archives; 73, Northwestern University Archives.

Index

Illustrations are indicated in italics. If a subject is illustrated and discussed on the same page, the illustration is not indicated separately.